PRAISE FOR
THE GIGACORN HUNTER

"Nelson Switzer knows first-hand how to spot and invest in companies and technologies that help tackle climate change. His excitement about the opportunity for anyone to invest for both impact and returns is inspiring, and it's only matched by his deep knowledge of markets and technologies. This book provides a concise, actionable guide for making meaningful investments in a rapidly changing world."

—Andrew Winston,
Best-Selling Author and
World-Renowned Sustainability Strategist

"The Gigacorn Hunter is an essential guide for anyone serious about climate investing. Nelson's unique blend of expertise in sustainability, finance, and strategy gives him the perfect perspective to write this book. He successfully bridges profitability with climate action, all while recognizing the immense scale of the challenge we face. This makes it a must-read for investors looking to navigate and thrive in the new economy."

—Dave Stangis,
Partner and Chief Sustainability Officer,
Apollo Capital Management

"If we're to solve the climate crisis, we'll need trillions in new investments across a broad range of technologies, sectors and geographies. It's an unprecedented opportunity, but one fraught with challenges. Thankfully, we have Nelson Switzer to lead us through the thicket. In his authoritative and imminently readable book he shows how climate solutions align with today's markets and tomorrow's future, and the potential value creation therein. This is a must-read for any professional investor, and anyone who strives for a better world."

—Joel Makower,
Chairman and Co-founder, Trellis Group

"In an era of government subsidies and regressive approaches to climate finance, Nelson Switzer brilliantly demonstrates that investment in climate action is not simply a sunk cost, but how it can drive exceptional returns. He masterfully condenses his decades of experience in technology and markets into an approach for climate investing that every investor should adopt. This book is a must-read, actionable guide for making profitable and meaningful investments in a rapidly changing world."

—Lisa DeMarco,
Senior Partner and CEO, Resilient LLP

"Nelson Switzer, an active seeker of climate solutions for nearly a quarter century, has much to share with investors, old and new, driven to put humanity on the path to net zero without sacrificing profits. Big profits. The stories within The Gigacorn Hunter will open your eyes, sharpen your perspective, and keep you both grounded and hopeful at a pivotal point in our collective climate fight."

—Tyler Hamilton,
Head of Climate, MaRS Discovery District

"The Gigacorn Hunter captures the reality that climate is the new economic revolution, reshaping industries and redefining opportunities. Nelson Switzer provides a practical guide to leading in this era, where addressing climate risk is not just a necessity but a pathway to unparalleled business growth. This book reflects the evolution of investments—where success is measured not only by financial returns but also by climate impact, such as carbon removed or mitigated. This essential read redefines what it means to be a business leader and is a must for anyone seeking to understand the forces shaping our future."

—Kookai Chaimahawong,
Executive Director, Centre for Climate and Business Solutions
at UBC Sauder School of Business

"This book is more than a guide—it's a wake-up call for investors to reimagine the power of their capital and lean in to shaping this new and important future. Nelson's narrative is bold, insightful, and profoundly inspiring, making this a must-read for anyone committed to building a sustainable and thriving world."

—**Michelle Scarborough,**
Managing Partner, Thrive Venture Fund and
Women in Tech Venture Fund, BDC Capital

"From the moment I first met Nelson I knew he was going to change the world for the better. Without fail, Nelson has delivered the strategy, the roadmap, and the infectious enthusiasm we need to meet the moment we've all anticipated when the market takes hold of our climate future delivering value to shareholders - both investors and humanity. What an exciting time to be alive and to become a Gigacorn Hunter!"

—**Dune Ives,**
Chief Marketing Officer, The Recycling Partnership
and Board Director, Ball Corporation

"Nelson Switzer's book illuminates the transformative shift we are experiencing—the electrification of transportation, the broader energy transition, and the societal changes these bring. By weaving together diverse perspectives and clear principles for investors, he reveals how profit, people, and planet can align rather than conflict. His emphasis on collaboration, even in the pursuit of competitive returns and decarbonization of the economy, is both timely and essential."

—**Anisa Kamadoli Costa,**
Chief Sustainability Officer, Rivian;
Trustee & President, Rivian Foundation

THE
GIGACORN
HUNTER

2

THE
GIGACORN

^{2}

HUNTER

Seven Principles for a
Climate Investor

Nelson Switzer

Published by
Hybrid Global Publishing
333 E 14th Street #3C New York, NY 10003

Manufactured in the United States of America, or the United Kingdom when distributed elsewhere.

Switzer, Nelson
The Gigacorn Hunter: Seven Principles for a Climate Investor
ISBN Hardcover: 978-1-967598-02-1
ISBN Paperback: 978-1-961757-84-4
eBook: 978-1-961757-87-5
LCCN: 2024924057

Cover design by: Julia Kuris
Copyediting by: Sue Toth
Interior design by: Amit Dey
Author photo by: Jenna Muirhead

Website: www.thegigacornhunter.com

Disclaimer

The information provided in this book is intended for entertainment and general informational purposes. Some stories reference real individuals and companies, while others have been adapted, fictionalized or amalgamated to illustrate broader principles and ideas. Readers are advised to consult with a licensed professional before making any investment decisions. The author and publisher assume no liability for financial outcomes resulting from actions based on the content of this book.

For Karen Lynne,
Noah Leaf
&
Ethan Rain

CONTENTS

THE GIGACORN HUNTER 2

THE PROFITS OF CLIMATE INVESTING

"Climate change is the single greatest threat to a sustainable future but, at the same time, addressing the climate challenge presents a golden opportunity to promote prosperity, security, and a brighter future for all."

— Ban-Ki Moon, former Secretary General UN

It has been said that the most important boardroom table is the breakfast table. It is where children ask their parents some of the most challenging questions: Deep mind and morality-bending questions. In our house, when my boys were a little younger, my youngest son, Ethan Rain, asked me this question:

"Dad, my teacher said that coal plants are causing climate change. What are you doing to stop them and help fix the climate?"

Finally! I had been waiting for years for someone to ask me that question…to give me an excuse, a reason to share.

For nearly 25 years, I've been bobbing and weaving in the fight to reverse climate change—listening and learning from friends, colleagues, and even those opposed to climate progress. I've taken my lumps and gathered my lessons. And those efforts have been more than a little rewarding—not only in learning how to slow and reverse the climate threats already plaguing the planet and threatening to worsen, but also in learning how to drive sustainable financial outcomes.

That's why my answer to my son's question is long—and it culminated in the writing of this book.

So, let me get started. Soapbox, please.

It is January 2012, and Enphase, a six-year-old clean energy startup, is preparing for its Initial Public Offering (IPO). If analyst projections are right, it will be the sort of home run, a grand slam actually, that we investors call a 2x Fund Returner: It will return double the whole of the original fund that invested in the company. Not just the investment made in the company, but the fund itself. Even if every other investment in the fund goes to zero and returns nothing, this fund is a success by virtue of the 2x fund returner that is about to be Enphase!

It's the kind of moment that turns fund managers into legends—wealthy legends.

The office is buzzing. Investment bankers, fund analysts, and associates shuffle about the office in organized chaos. A carefully choreographed modern dance production. Associates hammer at their keyboards, making last-minute tweaks to documents and presentations while calling out to their analysts, "You double-check that data yet?!" Dutiful junior analysts bounce from one desk to the other nervously confirming the quality of the data being fed into the machine that will turn out this victory.

Two conflicting aromas mingle in the air. There's the familiar welcome fragrance of eggs, bacon, and pancakes–the usual buffet laid out before the weekly Investment Team meetings—and the less-than-pleasant smell of body odor emanating from the armpits of bankers and analysts who worked through the night to ensure they got everything right for today's IPO.

It is an event that will change the lives of everyone with a financial stake in Enphase. More than that, it will change how power is generated–cleanly–for millions of people around the world and for decades to come.

The founders, venture capitalists (VCs), employees with stock options, and independent investors are bursting. They have big hopes that today will be a very good day.

Each has gambled financially with aspirations of large financial returns stemming from the company's unique technology that can help decarbonize the power grid and reduce the risks of climate change.

When they did the circuit, pitching investors and experts, the founders shared a vision that the company's unique microinverter technology could convert solar energy at the individual panel level, to reduce waste and carbon emissions while increasing energy efficiency, energy output, and sustainability.

Today, that vision will get a big shot of adrenaline.

For retail investors who dabble in the stock market, this IPO will bring them the opportunity to participate in the promise of Enphase. For those who did, it would catapult their investment from a share price of less than $8 per share in March 2012 to over $200 per share in March 2024, a return of more than 2,400 percent, many times more than the 2x Fund Returner that would have satisfied many of them.

From its very inception as a private company in 2006, Enphase has been on a mission to revolutionize the solar industry. With its unique microinverter technology, it connects to a solar panel and converts the direct current (DC) electricity generated by the panel into alternating current (AC) for use in homes or power grids.

They achieved this in remarkable fashion. With support of VCs such as Third Point Ventures, RockPort Capital Partners, Madrone Capital Partners, and Applied Ventures, Enphase has solidified its place as a major player in the cleantech, clean energy, and climate technology, or climatech, sectors.

By the end of 2023, Enphase's products were being used in over 3 million solar installations worldwide.[1] The company's share price success is based on profitability and growth in sales and profit margins, all of which is driven by market demand for solutions that decarbonize the power grid and help enterprises to access clean, renewable, low-cost electricity. Enphase's products and innovation have rapidly made solar power more affordable, removing a key obstacle to mass adoption. It is considered an important contributing reason why solar power is now the least expensive form of power generation worldwide.

Enphase demonstrated, whether by accident or design, a unique innovative investment model called climatech—a technology that enables the decarbonization of the economy, while delivering outstanding profits.

Enphase's founders and investors were among the early entrepreneurs to understand that the world needs to decarbonize and enabling that, the decarbonization of the economy, can produce significant profits. So, the founders built a business that does exactly that.

Other companies have done the same. They recognize that the mass market demand for decarbonization and the rapid transition to a net-zero economy have become huge drivers of economic activity. They see the same data we all see and understand that we have tipped over into a new paradigm where it is now more profitable to invest in companies that support a low-carbon future rather than those that drive atmospheric carbon intensity higher.

In short, it is now more profitable to invest in a sustainable future than contribute to global destruction.

Some of these companies focus on macro and system wide issues, while others focus on niche challenges. For example, Tesla dominates headlines with its solution for transportation, while companies such as Redwood Materials is expanding battery recycling and materials production to support the needs of all industries and segments such as land, sea, air travel, industrial systems, and grid-capacity storage. Still other players such as First Solar have figured out how to mass produce and deploy solar panels, while Recharge Industries is solving the intermittency challenges that come with solar and renewable power using battery storage. From Groundwork BioAg to MyLand, LineVision to Idlesmart, Mysa to Kuva, CleanFiber to Aqua Membrane, Membrion to Cyclic Materials, the list of companies pioneering solutions keeps getting longer and more viable.

As I write in the early months of 2024, there are more than one hundred such companies worth over a billion dollars each, and thousands more valued at over $100 million each. They are members of a new business category called climatech, short for climate technology. The term refers to innovative technologies and solutions designed to address climate change. It encompasses any technology, product, or service aimed at mitigating greenhouse gas emissions, either by preventing the release of these gases or facilitating the removal of it directly from the atmosphere (more on this later in Chapter 2) or reducing the unavoidable, physical impact of climate change.

More climatech companies are emerging every week. Each understands that now is the time to take a hard right turn away from fossil fuels and to reinvent the economy.

The Decarbonization of Everything

I call this new economic revolution, the Decarbonization of Everything (DoE). It is the era in which everything we depend upon to survive and thrive as a society must be reimagined and reinvented to ensure a low-carbon sustainable future, one that will be environmentally restorative, socially equitable, and economically prosperous. This decarbonization revolution will forge a path to wealth and health at an unprecedented scale and speed.

This shift is driven by five key trends:

1. Climatech solutions are cost-competitive with conventional solutions.
2. Demand for solutions that decarbonize corporations and their supply chains is remarkably sticky.
3. Regulation that supports and demands decarbonization is becoming deeply entrenched at the local, regional, national, and international levels.
4. Asset owners are experiencing losses and increased risks from the changing climate.
5. Carbon Dioxide in the atmosphere, the principal climate-regulating gas, is at an all–time high and climbing.

In the following chapters, I will explain how these trends form and how they enhance the demand for climatech innovations. But suffice it to say, climatech companies that solve business challenges, help customers manage risk, and create opportunity and value present exceptional investment opportunities.

Throughout this book, I will explore climatech companies, such as Enphase, which are transforming the kinds of investments that will return significant profits, while slowing, stabilizing, and hopefully, reversing climate change. VCs and private market investors will find climatech a unique and promising category for potential unicorns—companies that reach or exceed a billion dollars in market valuation.

Note this, however, climatech investors seek something more, something I call Gigacorns. These are companies that not only are worth over a billion dollars, but also will remove at least one billion tons of carbon from the economy.

Gigacorns will create the greatest number of high-paying jobs while mitigating the carbon legacy of the old economy. It is what we as investors seek—profits. And it is also what the world needs to survive, thrive and prosper—a stable environment with an abundance of natural resources to support life and the human compulsion to grow.

Climate Change Is Changing Your Life and Livelihood

Just as weather patterns become more unpredictable, your investment returns and opportunities may have become so as well.

For decades, you have been a successful investor. You've climbed a steep career path to reach your current stature as a fund manager, portfolio manager, corporate manager, institutional investor, family office manager, or everyday retail investor.

You've been trained in what works for your funds, your clients, and your portfolio. These methods have worked for decades, investing in such traditional categories as oil and gas, other natural resources, technology, biotech, insurance, and real estate.

But perhaps your ability to find value and deliver returns isn't quite what it used to be. The deals don't look so lucrative…and neither does your year-end bonus. Lately, your investment returns are down. Maybe you're writing off investments, looking to the future with trepidation instead of anticipation. Or maybe, your once-stable portfolio suddenly feels higher-risk than you can bare.

And maybe your daily activities and your very life have been different lately, too. Travel delays due to volatile and unpredictable weather events have disrupted your travel schedules. Floods, hurricanes, and tornadoes have rendered your home uninsurable. Even the availability and quality of the produce and groceries at your local market have become inconsistent at best.

You're not alone. Climate change is disrupting lives, business models, and investment portfolios everywhere. Now, more than ever, you see opportunities in adding climatech companies to your portfolio. You view this strategy not only as a hedge against lower returns—or worse, market collapse—but also as a path to spectacular profits and a more regulated climate.

Become a Climatech Investor

I have specialized in sustainable finance and climatech since 1999—as an environmental engineer, a banker, a corporate executive, an advisor, and an investor. I was a chief sustainability officer with Nestlé and Nestlé Waters, the senior manager of environmental affairs for the Royal Bank of Canada, and the former leader of the Sustainable Business Solutions practice for PWC, advising some of the world's largest pension plans, asset managers, corporations and governments.

As an early climatech investor, I've seen the rise of extraordinary opportunities–and failures.

I've tracked and worked to support this industry's rapid growth and championed some of the first socially responsible investment funds, launched the world's largest water fund, opened the first carbon trading desk in North America, advised some of the world's largest asset managers on environmental, social and governance (ESG) investment, diligence, and processes. I've diligenced hundreds and hundreds of potential investments and completed dozens of cleantech and climatech transactions.

At the end of 2019, I partnered with Kevin Kimsa and Paul Atkinson to co-found Climate Innovation Capital (ClimateIC), a venture fund that invests in solutions that deliver superior financial returns while simultaneously decarbonizing the economy as quickly as possible as we race against the climate clock. We call ourselves Gigacorn Hunters, because we seek out companies with the potential to exceed billion-dollar valuations while removing a billion tons of carbon from the economy.

This book crystallizes my experiences of the past twenty-five years to give you what you need to understand to become a climatech investor. I give you the foundation to kick off a successful investment strategy that can make you a wildly successful investor, simultaneously returning carbon to the earth and profits to your portfolio. I have codified my decades of experience into seven key principles to enlighten and delight you as an investor, seeker of profit, and climate mechanic.

These Seven Principles show you how to find, fund, and help grow climatech companies that return profit for you and reduce and remove carbon. Full credit to my fund partner Paul Atkinson who came up with that phrase...find, fund, and grow Gigacorns!

What Is a Climatech Investor?

Initially, I began this book for the Gigacorn Hunter and came to realize that while Gigacorn hunting was perhaps the fastest way to get to a net zero economy and a pre-industrial atmospheric concentration of carbon, that there was also room and necessity for other climatech investors such as Millicorn (thousand-ton reducers) and Megacorn (million-ton reducers) Hunters.

But why? The Intergovernmental Panel on Climate Change (IPCC) says the global community needs to remove fifty gigatons of carbon from the economy and at least ten billion tons from the atmosphere annually if we are to avoid the worst impacts of climate change.[2] So, if we just find sixty Gigacorns, doesn't that solve the problem? In theory, yes, but it's different in practice. Our economy is just not built in tidy billion carbon-ton slices.

Not every subsector emits a billion tons of carbon per year. So, if the economy must be decarbonized wholly, then there are a great many subsectors to decarbonize because they contribute hundreds of thousands or millions of tons of carbon. If we focus only on the technologies that can deliver a billion tons, we will miss important opportunities to deliver meaningful and necessary decarbonization and profit. I have not plotted it out on a graph or mapped it on a spreadsheet to determine the division of labor, but unquestionably, the decarbonization of the economy will require a diverse mix of exciting Millicorns, Megacorns, Gigacorns, and more.

Me? I am a Gigacorn Hunter. For me, the time for small moves is over. I am going to focus on the big moves, in the form of Gigacorn investments, that will provide inspiring examples to compel conventional capital off the bench and into climatech.

But there is room and the need for all sizes of climatech investors.

Whether you plan to be either a general climatech investor or a specialized Gigacorn Hunter, these seven principles offer a guiding framework. As each principle is laid bare, you will see into the decision-making process I have used over the years to make extraordinary profits for my employers and clients, and I provide many diverse examples.

If you follow these principles, you will be armed with a greater number of arrows in your investment quiver to hunt many opportunities offering the greatest returns and decarbonization potential. On top of that, you'll feel more prepared—even compelled—to divest yourself from investments that produce poor returns that continue to drive planetary, community, and economic destruction.

If you are an investment manager, you are poised to gain the most. You will move beyond skepticism to become a collaborative investment partner. Suppose you are a portfolio manager, chief investment officer, pension CEO, or an investment manager. In that case, you will see bigger paychecks and bonuses, better career longevity, legacy wealth, and the respect that comes from being among the first to pave the way to a new and better normal.

As a professional investor, you can invest either institutional capital or personal funds, or you can build a new fund or other investment vehicle. You may have the critical skill and expertise to join another fund or have the ability to influence those who have the capital to invest. If you want to start your own fund, you can recruit people who show the potential to become Gigacorn Hunters for you.

If you're an entrepreneur looking to raise equity from a VC firm, you're going to understand how to appeal to Gigacorn Hunters who are following the seven principles. You'll be able to shape your story more effectively to encourage the capital that's transitioning out of the old economy and into the new.

If you're a business or MBA student aspiring to manage money in your future career, you will gain a valuable education into the deepest opportunity for investment returns and decarbonization of the economy. If you're a pensioner or approaching retirement, this book will provide you with talking points for your asset managers about climatech investing.

Or, if you are a retail investor, you can use these seven principles to identify private and public companies that can grow into Gigacorns. Just as Enphase and Tesla were small unicorns when they debuted on the stock market, you can identify new listings and invest in the climatech Gigacorns of the future.

No matter what type of investor you are, these Seven Principles will help you become a more informed and effective investor. You can choose companies that deliver exceptional financial returns, while generating environmental and social prosperity.

By following these principles, you can upend your portfolio and reinvest in stronger, better-returning companies set to decarbonize and grow our shared future. You become empowered to both steward and benefit from the transition to a low-carbon economy.

Blazing the Path

Climatech investors are no longer a fringe, no longer a niche. It is no longer a choice between profit and purpose or between money and climate. We now have both. We can be climate capitalists and seize the opportunity to invest in an industry that can restore and sustain our planet and our communities…and make us a phenomenal amount of money while we're at it.

If your passion is profit, this book is for you. If your purpose is decarbonizing the economy and sustainable development, this book is for you as well.

After absorbing my Seven Principles, you will have the confidence to choose companies that can produce solid returns for your fund or portfolio, enhancing the likelihood of your long-term success and financial gain. But more than that, you will be recognized as a pioneering investor who saw the future and acted. Your legacy begins now.

CHAPTER 1

THE DECARBONIZATION OF EVERYTHING

"If you really think the environment is less important than the economy, try holding your breath while you count your money."

— Guy McPherson, Professor Emeritus of natural resources and ecology and evolutionary biology at the University of Arizona

The telltale signs of economic revolution are flashing brightly. They include political, employment, energy, and economic signals such as a rapid shift in the political fodder used to sway the masses, a quick tightening of the job market with increasingly complex skills required to fill employer needs, an intensifying need for energy and, of course, rapid economic growth.

Does this sound familiar? It should, because we are at the beginning of a new economic revolution—the fifth, which I call the Decarbonization of Everything (DoE).

Economic revolutions are ignited by innovations that disrupt how we do things–and that is what is happening with the DoE, and climatech. Since the mid-1700s, civilization has undergone four major economic transformations, each marked by a shift toward a new energy source.

They are:

1. **The Mechanical Revolution (1765).** Society moved from agriculture as the main driver of wealth toward industrial manufacturing, powered by coal and steam—pushing and pulling machines in factories, and locomoting iron horses across continents.

2. **The Motorized Revolution (1870).** Society shifted to mass adoption of the internal combustion engine, chemical processes, and the telephone. It was powered by fossil fuels including oil and gas, and supplemented by electricity, a major new source of power.

3. **The Electronics Revolution (1960).** The addition of nuclear energy to the fossil fuel fray transformed how we work and live with electronics, telecommunications, and computers running on a massive incremental electricity supply.

4. **The Internet Revolution (1998).** The internet reshaped how we access, process, and bend information. While the energy supply remained largely unchanged, the mix of fuel sources shifted as demand for energy and electricity grew substantively as countries like Brazil, Russia, India and China clawed their way up the ladder of economic development and the global population swelled.

5. **The Decarbonization of Everything Revolution (2018).** Climatech entered the mainstream as society recognized the need to reinvent everything in the economy so it emits either no- or low-carbon—and the need to remove legacy carbon that remains in the atmosphere. There is a concerted global effort to minimize or eliminate the burning of fossil fuels and felling of massive forests that has endured throughout the last 250 years of industrialization, driving the greenhouse effect from the atmosphere. This era is marked also by the electrification of the economy and is powered by renewable energy. There is a global movement to retire fossil fuels such as oil, gas, and coal.

With each successive revolution, or transformation, the wealth creation opportunity grew exponentially larger, while the period of opportunity tightened.

Compare the value of railroad tycoons of the 1800s to the wealth creation of internal combustion automotive companies in the 1900s and the electric vehicle (EV) companies of today. The scale of wealth created grows greater with each successive transformation, while the time to generate wealth during each transformation has become shorter. This is evidenced by how quickly we are moving into the fifth revolution, the DoE.

There is another reason the economic opportunity of the DoE will eclipse the size and scale of any previous revolution. Every first-year physics, chemistry, or general science student knows and understands the second law of thermodynamics, Entropy. In short, it states that the universe tends toward expansion and disorder. It is why we cannot unscramble an egg. To reverse Entropy requires a multiple of energy input, much of which will be lost in the unscrambling process. When we apply this law to the DoE, the results are staggering. Civilization has spent hundreds of years developing systems to pump, process and burn fossil fuels, to fell forests and shape our civilization and economy to one reliant on these systems. Now we must reverse this process—in total contravention of the second law of thermodynamics. That's going to cost us. It is always harder to put the genie back in the bottle.

Climatech Solutions

When raising Fund I for ClimateIC, I repeatedly heard statements like, "I knew someone who invested in cleantech in 2006, and they lost it all," and "I lost a bundle investing in cleantech in 2013. Why would I take on that risk again?"

That's the right question—and there are good answers.

According to data from Cambridge Associates, Cleantech Group, and others, an estimated $50 billion was invested in Cleantech between

2000 and 2015 to solve environmental problems such as renewable energy, energy efficiency, electric vehicles (EVs), batteries, and green chemistry.[3] The problem was that market demand for such solutions was nascent at best. Was it the ethical thing to do? From an environmental perspective, absolutely. But was it a good investment? As we will discuss, no, it was not–at least not at that time.

So, what changed? COP21 and the signing of The Paris Accord happened. It was a global commitment to limit climate change to less than two degrees Celsius and was signed by 196 governments.[4] It removed barriers for corporations, regulators, investors, and entrepreneurs.

Think of it this way: Before COP 21, the climatech investment level exceeded the demand for the solutions being developed, causing many start-up companies to fail. Post-COP 21, there was a crossing of trendlines. Suddenly, demand far exceeded the investment level into climatech. Private capital and climate entrepreneurs saw this and began cooperating to fill this previously unfunded opportunity. And there remains a lot of room to run.

In fact, according to PriceWaterhouseCoopers, by 2022 the market for climatech surpassed $2.5 trillion and is expected to exceed $4 trillion by 2025.[5] The United Nations Framework Convention on Climate Change (UNFCCC) and the International Monetary Fund pegs the climatech investment opportunity at more than $125 trillion by 2050.[6] McKinsey, the leading global consultancy, estimates it to be closer to $250 trillion.[7]

If you need more proof, climatech data from PricewaterhouseCoopers (PwC) 2023 State of Climate Tech and the 2023 Money Tree Report from PwC and the National Venture Capital Association, reported that climatech had grown its share of all private investment from approximately 1.4 percent to nearly 11.5 percent by 2023.[8,9]

The cherry on top is data from CB Insights, Pitchbook, and Silicon Valley Bank, now owned by First Citizen's Bank. It reports climatech investments to be more resilient than conventional tech investments, indicating that climatech is sustaining valuations more readily than conventional tech investments, even during recessions.[10,11,12] Since 2023 the industry appears to have had the fastest emergence of unicorns—companies whose valuations exceed $1 billion, according to HolonIQ, a global market intelligence platform focused on climate, education, and healthcare investments.[13]

Either way, the opportunity is extraordinary, the opportunity for profit and sustainable outcomes for people and the planet.

Five Trends Driving the DoE

But what gave governments and corporations worldwide the courage to finally commit to addressing climate change? I see five major trends:

Trend #1. Climatech solutions are cost-competitive with conventional solutions.

There has been a persistent myth that environmentally responsible products don't perform as well as traditional counterpart products that cost less. This certainly used to be the case, but no more. Now, climatech solutions not only perform as well or better than conventional solutions, but they are also cost competitive, priced at the same or lesser cost.

Consider this: The levelized cost of electricity (LCOE), a common tool used to measure and compare the lifetime cost of generating electricity from power plants, of solar power plants is lower than virtually any other power source in almost every region of the world.[14] Innovation in solar technology and economies of scale have made this a reality.

Moreover, this advance comes while oil, gas, and coal producers gobbled up nearly $1 trillion in annual subsidies as of 2022.[15] This is turning heads not just in retail, but also among corporate consumers who are increasingly driven by both cost efficiency and corporate social responsibility goals.

If you are looking for a more consumer-facing product, please consider the common light bulb. Not long ago, the LED bulb was an expensive solution with a harsh, unnatural glow. Now, they cost the same or less as incandescent bulbs (if you can even find them anymore), and LEDs come in a variety of colors and brightness, with the ability to dim as you would an incandescent bulb. The LED has become a drop-in replacement that uses six to ten times less electricity and lasts up to twenty-one times longer, offering lower upfront and operating costs.[16]

Surveys show that a growing number of retail consumers are influenced by environmental impact in their purchasing decisions.[17] As awareness increases, so does the demand for sustainable products that don't sacrifice quality or cost-effectiveness. On the other hand, corporate customers are motivated by long-term savings, energy efficiency, and the growing importance of sustainable practices for favorable brand image and investor relations.

When an innovation disrupts a conventional technology in performance and/or price, the law of economic gravity takes hold. And, in an era where individual consumers and large corporations increasingly prioritize sustainability, climate-smart products that offer superior performance and cost savings are no longer just an alternative: they are the first choice.

Trend #2: Demand for solutions that decarbonize corporations, institutions, and their supply chains is remarkably sticky.

There is a deeply entrenched demand for decarbonization by corporations, institutions, and their supply chains. It is driven by a confluence of factors ranging from the tangible climate change impacts to the evolving expectations of consumers, investors, and regulators. Significant initiatives from leading companies are evidence of this trend.

For example, Amazon has not only created a $10 billion climate fund, but also reinforced its commitment by naming its new Seattle event center Climate Pledge Arena, reflecting the growing demand for environmentally responsible business practices.[18] Similarly, Microsoft's pledge to net-zero emissions from their operations and all emissions since their founding, backed by a substantial billion-dollar fund, underscores the increasing importance that investors place on sustainable practices and climate strategies.[19]

These actions are part of a broader movement where businesses do not just respond to immediate pressure but are proactively shaping sustainable futures. Walmart's ambitious Gigaton Challenge, aimed at eliminating a billion tons of greenhouse gas emissions by 2030, demonstrates how companies can influence their entire supply chain toward more sustainable practices, responding to demands from customers and partners with strong climate action commitments.[20]

Moreover, the shift toward renewable energy and energy-efficient technologies isn't solely driven by environmental considerations. It also offers long-term cost savings, crucial for maintaining competitiveness in a market where resource efficiency is key.

Finally, reputation is increasingly at the forefront of corporate strategies. The emergence of the Task Force on Climate-related Financial Disclosures (TCFD) as a critical climate risk disclosure tool is compelling corporations to assess and transparently report how they manage climate risk. This moves toward greater transparency and accountability in climate action, enhances corporate reputation, fosters trust among stakeholders and aligns with the broader shift toward sustainability and environmental stewardship in the business world.

The persistent demand for decarbonization solutions is a multifaceted phenomenon, rooted in economic, environmental, and social drivers, compelling companies to integrate these solutions into their core strategies for resilience and long-term success.

These changes are converging into a massive opportunity for corporate, institutional and retail investors to solve the climate crisis while simultaneously enjoying significant investment returns.

Trend #3: Regulations that support decarbonization are deeply entrenched at all levels.

Regulations supporting or requiring decarbonization are shaping a new era where environmental consciousness is not only encouraged, but mandated.

Globally, governments are intensifying regulatory measures that encompass a broad spectrum of initiatives. States, provinces, and nations are setting rigorous car emission limits and standards, defining precise pollution allowances and, along with international bodies, are committing to ambitious carbon emission reduction targets.

These laws increasingly favor carbon-innovative products and services over traditional, high-carbon options, marking a pivotal shift in legislative focus.

The US Inflation Reduction Act and Canada's Growth Fund exemplify significant legislative efforts supporting clean technology and a low-carbon future. The European Union's Carbon Cap-and-Trade system incentivizes businesses to reduce emissions, and the EU Green Deal, represents a comprehensive initiative to transform the EU into a modern, resource-efficient economy. Internationally, the trend to phase away from internal combustion engines is accelerating, with countries like France aiming for 2040 and India targeting 2030 for a complete transition to electric vehicles (EVs).[21]

These measures illustrate the legal underpinnings of a global shift in transportation policies.

The motivation behind this regulatory change is the social license granted to governments, powered by the proven viability of climatech solutions as alternatives to traditional technologies.

A highly visible example of this is Elon Musk's role in demonstrating EVs as not only suitable, but also cost-effective alternatives to internal combustion engines (ICE). This has led to a surge in legislation favoring EVs. Countries such as Norway, targeting an ICE passenger vehicle ban by 2025, the UK aiming for 2030, and other jurisdictions like California and the Netherlands, are examples.[22]

The question of "why now?" is answered by the convergence of technological innovation, public awareness, and climate concern. Climatech solutions has evolved to a point where it often outperforms traditional alternatives. Governments are responding to an increasingly climate-concerned populace, aligning technological feasibility with public demand. This synergy has set the stage for ambitious regulatory frameworks that guide the global community toward a sustainable, low-carbon future.

This does not mean there are not exceptional pressures applied to governments and stakeholders to preserve the old economy. Transitions are always chaotic, but when governments finally design policies to change paths, the winners of the past may no longer find themselves on the podium and will work to claw their way back on top.

What is happening now is the regulatory landscape for decarbonization reflecting a global consensus shaped by technological advancements and a societal mandate for climate action. It's a dynamic amalgamation of innovation, public advocacy, and strategic legislation, all converging to steer the world toward a more sustainable, prosperous, and climate-stable future.

Trend #4: Asset owners are experiencing losses and greater risks from the changing climate.

You've seen the headlines: wildfires in the United States, Canada, Greece, Australia and Italy, drought in Brazil and the American Southwest, super-floods in Beijing and Alaska, famine in Somalia, and more.[23] The human and business implications of these events are profound, with financial losses reshaping industries on a global scale.

In Canada, the 2023 wildfire season resulted in significant financial losses. The Insurance Bureau reported billions in claims, impacting sectors like mining, forestry, and housing.[24] In California, wildfires led to PG&E, the state's privately run utility, filing for bankruptcy, with liabilities exceeding $30 billion due to its role in sparking wildfires, a grim testament to the financial impact of climate-induced disasters.[25] Utility companies worldwide are similarly vulnerable, with lawsuits and financial losses from climate-induced disasters.

Considering that large institutional investors such as Berkshire Hathaway and pension funds like CalSTRS, OMERS and Norway's Government Pension Fund are some of the most prolific investors in climate vulnerable utilities and infrastructure, the impact of on pensioners, and pending and current retirees is staggering.

The oil and gas industry faces its own set of challenges, particularly with stranded assets. Major players like Royal Dutch Shell have recognized that many of their reserves can't be developed if the world is to meet climate commitments, leading to significant financial losses. In 2021, Shell announced approximately $22 billion of reserve asset write-downs, a substantial financial acknowledgment of the changing energy landscape.[26]

Real estate values, particularly in coastal areas, are declining due to rising sea levels caused by climate change, causing a drop in property values and investment attractiveness globally.

In agriculture and food industries, volatile weather, higher temperatures, and migrating insects are causing increased costs and supply chain disruptions. Companies like Coca-Cola and Nestlé have highlighted these challenges in their annual reports, pointing to adverse financial implications.[27, 28]

The unpredictability of traditional investments in a climate-impacted world is leading to a shift in the investment landscape. The emergence of climate investment funds is a key indicator of this transition. Incumbents like Brookfield Asset Management launched a $15 billion Global Transition Fund, and TPG unleashed a $7.3 billion Rise Climate Fund, and firms like Union Square Ventures, are establishing significant climatech funds.[29, 30] New players like Chris Sacca's Lower Carbon Capital are also making their mark. Lower Carbon Capital raised $800 million, showcasing the growing interest in climatech-focused investments.[31]

Additionally, the collaborative fund, Decarbonization Partners, between BlackRock and Temasek of Singapore further underscores this trend, with substantial fund sizes of more than $1.4 billion indicating the scale of commitment to climatech investing at scale.[32]

Investors globally and the citizenry alike are demanding a transformation in capital markets and business behavior, pushing for investments in companies that actively contribute to a low-carbon future. This shift isn't just about environmental stewardship; it's a strategic move toward ensuring profitability in a world where climate change is a defining factor in economic stability and growth. This is the essence of climate capitalism—leveraging traditional capital for investments that are both environmentally sound and economically viable.

Trend #5: Carbon Dioxide in the atmosphere, the principal climate-regulating gas, is at an all–time high and climbing.

In the pre-industrial days of the late 1700s, the concentration of carbon dioxide in the atmosphere hovered around 280 parts per million (ppm) or less. By 2023, this figure had dramatically escalated to 421 ppm.[33] This rapid, significant increase is mainly attributable to two forces: the combustion of fossil fuels like oil, gas, and coal, and widespread deforestation. The burning of these fossil fuels increases the rate of carbon emissions, while the loss of forests also reduces the capacity of the natural environment to absorb carbon dioxide, disrupting the delicate balance of the natural carbon cycle.

The impact of these two forces has contributed to the volatile climate conditions that humanity is witnessing. The inability to predict weather patterns and the increasing severity of events like floods, droughts, wildfires, snow melts, hurricanes, tornadoes, avalanche, and more are wreaking havoc on infrastructure, communities, and ecosystems alike. This results in significant disruptions to critical systems, including power, supply chains, communication, and transportation.

As the concentration of carbon in the atmosphere reaches new records, the associated risks continue to climb. Excessive carbon dioxide in the atmosphere is trapping heat, as if it were a blanket wrapped around the Earth. This trapped heat causes weather patterns to change, leading to a variety of environmental and societal impacts. For example, the Thwaites Glacier, a massive 470-kilometer-long glacier above the Arctic Ocean, is melting at an alarming rate.[34] Its collapse could lead to a significant rise in sea levels worldwide, flooding and destroying shoreline cities.

Other major climate trends include the expanding Azores High, an atmospheric high-pressure ridge over the North Atlantic affecting rainfall and drought across Europe.[35] In the US, drought has led to severe reductions in water levels in lakes and reservoirs like Lake Mead, disrupting power production.[36] The melting Arctic permafrost is destroying infrastructure built on what was once permanently frozen ground.[37]

The emergence of new diseases is another climate change symptom. Rising temperatures release new bacteria from the melting permafrost, and cause insects and rodents to migrate to new regions, bringing new pathogens and increasing the region in which viruses spread.[38] This leads to mass pandemics and diseases as indicators of climate volatility.

Food insecurity is another growing concern. Rising temperatures and volatile water availability are making it increasingly difficult to produce sufficient food. Crop failures cause food shortages in some countries, while others ban food exports to feed their populations, leading to dramatic rises in food prices.[39]

Migration is a direct consequence of these changes. Without energy, food, and housing security, people move to areas with better resources, leading to refugee crises and conflicts.

The Mission

As climatech investors, our mission is to find and finance companies that emit no or low carbon. Ideally, we would sequester carbon from the atmosphere too, thus reversing the global warming trend. That's why progressive climate investors look for companies capable of removing at least one billion tons of carbon from the economy and the atmosphere.

The World Meteorological Organization reported that from 1970 to 2021, there were 12,000 extreme weather events that killed more than two million people and caused over $4.3 trillion of damage.[40] As weather grows more extreme, these numbers are predicted to rise, emphasizing the urgency for climatech innovation and investment. It also tells us that the math is currently upside down. Investing in the decarbonization of the economy now is much cheaper than waiting. The longer we wait, the more extreme the costs—in life and property damage.

The climatech transformation rides these five trends and are creating tremendous investment opportunities for those who can identify the companies most capable of solving climate challenges that solve business challenges—and deliver superior returns.

The DoE is giving rise to a new generation of climate investors, an elite breed known as Gigacorn Hunters, as I will explain in the next chapter.

GREENHOUSE GAS 101

Carbon is an element on the periodic table like gold, hydrogen or oxygen. **Carbon** is also common shorthand for **Carbon Dioxide (CO_2)** or **Carbon Dioxide Equivalents (CO_2e)**, the reference term for molecules that contribute to climate change. These molecules are also known as **Greenhouse Gases (GHGs)**, each with its own **Global Warming Potential (GWP)**. A GWP of one (1) represents the climate impact of one (1) molecule of Carbon Dioxide.

Carbon (Greenhouse Gases)	Global Warming Potential (100-year time horizon)
Carbon Dioxide (CO_2)	1
Methane (CH_4)	28
Nitrous Oxide (N_2O)	265
Sulphur Hexafluoride (SF_6)	23,500
Nitrogen Trifluoride (NF_3)	16,100
Hydrofluorocarbons (HFCs)	12-17,400

GHGs are also divided into different categories known as Scopes. The Scope of GHG emissions is one of the more important topics in GHG Accounting. It helps establish the boundaries of emissions. Boundaries refer to what emissions are to be included in any particular GHG inventory. This helps ensure identification of the accountable and responsible party, prevents double-counting and ensures emissions coverage.

Scope 1 - Direct emissions from owned or controlled sources.

Example: fuels consumed to fire boilers, air conditioners and equipment on site. Refrigerant leaks are also included here.

Scope 2 - Indirect emissions from the purchase of energy.

Example: electricity consumed by the user, which power is produced offsite, such as coal, natural gas or diesel power.

Scope 3 - Indirect emissions that occur in the value chain.

Example: emissions resulting from raw materials, procurement, manufacture, sale, logistics, use and disposal of products.

CHAPTER 2

THE FIRST GIGACORN HUNTER

"A long time ago, when the earth was still green
And there were more kinds of animals than you've ever seen
They'd run around free while the earth was being born
But the loveliest of all was the unicorn...."

— Shel Silverstein, poet, folk singer

In 2018, I sat on a Milken Institute conference panel where I shared my perspectives on climate change and investing. Afterward, I was approached by an affluent and storied family of three from Atlanta who had many questions about how to qualify an investment as climate-positive, where to find these opportunities, and how to understand the scale of their impact.

The youngest asked me, "So, are you hunting for climate unicorns?"

That was the right question, but I hadn't realized it yet. I asked him to explain. "A climate unicorn has a positive impact on climate change," he told me.

A unicorn startup is a venture-backed company that has achieved a valuation of over $1 billion. The term, first coined in 2013 by Aileen Lee, a Silicon Valley VC, was apt, because such startups are as elusive as the mythical creatures that are impossible to find or catch.[41]

The unicorn terms remain in use by investors, even though they are not as elusive today as they once were. According to CBInsights, a market intelligence firm, as of 2023, there were more than 1,200 unicorns in the US.[42] They include many companies you know, such as Meta, Airbnb, LinkedIn, Stripe, OpenAI, Grammarly, Uber, and SpaceX.

Knowing that a billion tons of carbon is referred to as a Gigaton, the contraction felt natural. Gigaton plus Unicorn equals Giga-corn.

And there it was. Inspired by this young man's question, I coined the term Gigacorn to describe the companies I want to invest in. They are startups with the potential to exceed $1 billion valuations while avoiding or removing at least a billion tons of carbon.

At that moment, I believe I became the first monikered Gigacorn Hunter.

Climatech investing is clearly an idea whose time has come. The world's collective consciousness is calling for a new breed of investors, arguably the most ambitious of us being Gigacorn Hunters.

We Gigacorn Hunters are climate optimists. We see great promise in the environmental, social, and economic challenges we face. We believe that the climate problems we face can be solved. By investing in companies that focus and have the potential to reach Gigacorn status, we empower companies with the resources to develop and market technologies that drive the transition to a low-carbon economy, to the DoE.

Massive Opportunity

As I mentioned, the entire economy must be reinvented if we are to decarbonize the world. As my partner at ClimateIC, Kevin Kimsa likes to say, "Everything must be reimagined, reengineered, and reinvented." Everything we use for work, travel, and recreation must be reconceived: buildings, cars, trucks, factories, farms. Nothing is off the table.

With each challenge comes the potential to create Gigacorns that generate billions of dollars of market, commercial, community and environmental value. There is plenty of space for every investment nickel that will produce superior returns.

Right now, there are so many climatech investment opportunities with the potential to become Gigacorns, or even Megacorns (million-ton potential) and Decacorns (10 billion ton potential) but the capacity to fund them remains limited. Funds like mine, ClimateIC, surely can't fill them all. As of early 2024, there were over 1185 dedicated or associated climate investment funds worldwide, and together we haven't even come close to funding all the potential and necessary Gigacorns worldwide.[43]

At ClimateIC, our team researches more than 500 companies annually, and we finance less than 1 percent of them. We only invest in companies we believe are potential Gigacorns. As a growth-oriented fund, our investments must also have existing commercial sales and show scalable growth. Across our investment portfolio, we anticipate 2.5 times the return on cash and a 25 percent internal-rate-of-return (IRR).

This financial return is the primary reason we founded ClimateIC. We believe that by demonstrating to conventional investors that climate returns are as good or better than conventional investing, we will draw that capital off the sidelines and out of the conventional, or old economy, to accelerate the pace of the DoE transition, to a low-carbon economy.

A Data-Driven Moral Code

I am driven by two powerful forces. The first is a reliance on research and data. The second is the edict of *tikkun olam*, a Jewish precept instilled in me from a young age that requires me, as a Jewish person, to try to repair and improve the world.

My education began in science and shifted to engineering, business and investing. This journey led me to evolve into a business strategist. I spend my time gathering, questioning, understanding, and analyzing data that shape my decisions.

Over twenty-five years, that data has told me that climatech investing and Gigacorn hunting will deliver the highest financial returns while simultaneously changing the course of civilization in a direction that is environmentally, socially, and economically beneficial: A tidy match between my moral code and the data.

Inspired by Seaweed

I've met thousands of people who play various roles in the climate change ecosystem. From investors to entrepreneurs, regulators to NGOs. The cast of characters is extensive and diverse. But we share one thing in common: we are compelled to connect with nature.

If you happen to be a climatech investor, you may have a story, or experience, that transformed your life, such as gardening with your grandparents as a child, eating fresh berries off the bush, taking a class on climate change, or being questioned at the dinner table by one of your children about what you are doing to ensure your grandchildren will have a safe, healthy, prosperous planet to inhabit and inherit.

This is my story.

My grandfather encouraged me as a child to become a doctor. He didn't care what kind of doctor, so long as it was in the medical category.

As a dutiful grandson, I started in the direction he set for me, but I was also drawn in other directions, toward nature, where I developed a passion early in life that were refined and deepened during my summers camping and canoeing in Ontario's Algonquin Provincial Park.

With a love for nature and a need to complete a science degree to qualify for medical school, I attended the University of New Brunswick, where I had the chance to study at the Huntsman Marine Center on the shores of the North Atlantic Ocean.

In the summer between my second and third year, I took the class that would change my life—marine botany, the study of marine algae.

The sea set a rhythm to my days. I would wake up at low tide, collect intertidal and tidal zone samples, head back to the lab, categorize my samples, return to the shoreline at low tide nearly twelve hours later, eat, drink, or sleep, and then repeat.

One time, as my classmates and I were drinking long into the night, someone posed a challenge to see who could lay face down on the beached seaweed the longest as the tide came in.

Two of us took up the challenge.

We all went tripping down to the beach so early that it was still dark to catch low tide. The wide flat expanse of gray sand was covered with a beautiful dark green seaweed called *Ascophyllum nodosum*. Each strand was capped with a series of little balloon-like vesicles. The seaweed stretched across the rocky shoreline and was piled a few feet high.

Laughing and stumbling on the seaweed, I stepped out of my tall rain boots and yanked off my heavy wool sweater. I then laid face down on the seaweed, shivering in my t-shirt. There wasn't much water yet, but it was the North Atlantic. Even in summer, the water is freezing, and I could feel little critters moving around in the seaweed beneath me.

There we were, two drunk idiots in the seaweed, our classmates and friends nearby cackling at us. There was not a cloud in the slowly lightening sky. Their chortles faded away as I became filled with calm.

Lying there, my head exposed to the water's edge creeping closer. I tilted my head to watch the approaching tide, and saw sea urchins attached to rocks, with sea cucumbers out further: And then came the tide.

Most people may envision the tide as a big rush of water, but it's not. It rolls in sheets, one on top of the other. They layer and build one on top of the next.

At that moment, the sun appeared over the horizon and irradiated everything. I saw stacks of glowing red, green, and blue algae, layered over and over in sequence. The beauty, organization, and cooperation moved me. Suddenly, I realized how delicately codependent all the living things in our ecosystem were.

I thought, "What change am I causing to the ecosystem right now because I'm lying here? What change is the Marine Center forcing on the shoreline? What changes are the fisheries down the bay imposing? And what changes are forced upon the ocean from global industrial activity?" I was hooked as a great unlock of curiosity enveloped me.

In that moment I thought, "Sorry Grandpa. Forget med school. This is what I'm going to study."

I parleyed an undergraduate degree in biology into a Master of Environmental Engineering focusing on Sustainable Development obtaining also a sub-specialty in Environmental Studies. It was here that I chiseled out what would become my purpose. I would seek to leverage the capital markets to solve the world's biggest challenges with climate change being foremost.

Sustainable Development: meeting current needs without compromising the ability of future generations to meet their own needs–Brundtland Commission Report, Section 3, Paragraph 27, the most cited definition of sustainable development. The statement I admire more is found three paragraphs down. It says sustainable development is a process of change in which the direction of investments, the orientation of technological development, and institutional change are made consistently with future as well as present needs.[44]

Climatech and climate investing fit squarely into that rarely cited passage.

An Impatient Career in Sustainability

I have worked as an environmental engineer, a banker, an energy executive, a consultant, a Chief Sustainability Officer, and an investor. I've learned various lessons about business, management, and people from each position, but none more clearly than this one about myself: I am impatient. If a company does not want to immediately change, and work to become sustainable, it probably never will, and it is best for me to move on to a place where my skills can drive value. If someone argues against the DoE, I will go around them. In all likelihood, they will go the way of the Dodo.

But there is another side. Like me, the climate is impatient.

It is this complementary impatience between my character and the climate that compels me professionally.

Six Days to $20 Million

Throughout my many vocations, I think I have learned how to communicate. I have crafted a management approach that helps business decision makers see opportunities, manage risks and leverage their strengths. I have invested in dozens of projects that produced returns ranging from zero to ten times.

Prior to co-founding ClimateIC, I advised and was recruited by institutional asset managers in Canada, the US, Europe, and Australia.

In November 2019, my friend Phil Haid, someone I admire greatly for his commitment to purpose, impact and sustainability as well as his intellect, humor and nature, introduced me to Kevin Kimsa and Paul Atkinson, who would soon partner with me to co-found ClimateIC. Having been partners for more than thirty years, Kevin and Paul were responsible for Canada's first tech unicorn. It was also Canada's largest tech exit, a distinction they enjoyed for more than twenty years.

Following that success, they founded several additional companies and spent much time investing in and as VCs: Kevin is the founder of

ScaleUP Ventures, and Paul is chairman of the Investment Committee of Imperial Capital.

When I met them, they were seeking to transition into climatech investing and were motivated by a sense of urgency about climate and an awareness of their investment and operational skills.

We had planned a one-hour meeting to discuss working together. It lasted all morning.

Toward the end, I took the time to summarize what we had discussed. It is a habit I picked up as a consultant. I drew a three-axis plot and labeled them money, carbon, and time. Then, I drew a sphere at the top right of the plot and said, "We want to invest in solutions that can deliver the highest rate of return and the greatest decarbonization in the shortest period of time."

The Climate Investor Strategy

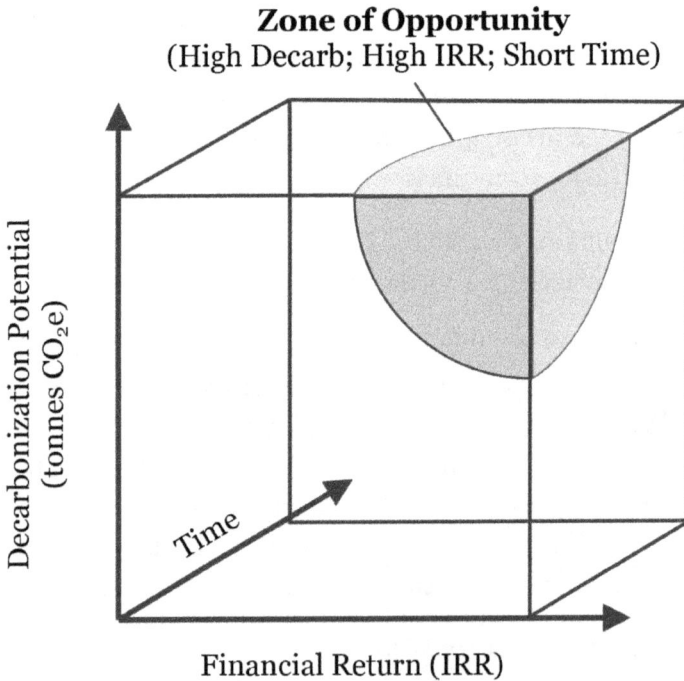

Zone of Opportunity
(High Decarb; High IRR; Short Time)

Decarbonization Potential (tonnes CO_2e)

Time

Financial Return (IRR)

"That's it! That's how we need to frame this. That is what we need to do," Paul and Kevin chimed in.

We spent the next few months discussing ideas and concepts, to augment conventional forms of technology venture investing.

We had to ensure that we could account for the carbon impact, and we had to overcome the myth that a fund like ours couldn't be profitable. We had to prove that we would see the same or better returns than conventional funds and that we could create value beyond the decarbonization benefits.

After crafting key thoughts and completing research, it was clear we had not yet fully leaned in, so I proposed that we give ourselves six weeks to raise $15 million. If we could do that, we would know we were onto something. We would shut everything else down and focus on building a climatech fund.

We agreed. Six days later we had raised $20 million.

We formed Climate Innovation Capital, or ClimateIC as everyone calls us, and it immediately became our full-time commitment. We raised $100 million for our first fund and assembled a team of eight Gigacorn Hunters.

We focus on opportunities from all six sectors of the economy that are responsible for all anthropogenic (human-induced) carbon emissions. These include, energy power and storage, transportation and mobility, industrial processes and management, agriculture, buildings, waste plastic and recycling.

The Six Sectors of the Economy

Energy, Power Generation & Storage

Food, Agriculture & Forestry

Transportation & Mobility

Sectors

Buildings

Industrial Processes & Products

Waste, Plastic & Recycling

Sectors:

Energy, Power Generation & Storage: The ability to source, transform and deliver reliable, high-quality energy. *~30% (or 15 GT of CO_2e) of annual global emission.*

Transportation & Mobility: The efficient movement of people and goods locally, regionally and globally. *~15% (or 8 GT of CO_2e) of annual global emission.*

Industrial Processes & Management: The extraction, transformation, and manufacture of goods required to meet society's needs. *~27% (or 13 GT of CO_2e) of annual global emission.*

Food, Agriculture & Forestry: The growth, harvest, processing, and provision of nourishment to feed, clothe, and house society. *~18% (or 9 GT of CO_2e) of annual global emission.*

Buildings: The design, construction, and operation of residential, commercial and industrial space. *~6% (or 3 GT of CO_2e) of annual global emission.*

Waste, Plastic & Recycling: The collection, transportation, sorting, treatment, reuse, and disposition of products. ~3% (or 2 GT of CO_2e) of annual global emission.

As Gigacorn Hunters, we seek solutions that aggressively decarbonize the economy by at least one billion tons. Toward this goal, we embrace my seven key principles for climate investing and Gigacorn hunting, which I explain in the next chapter.

CHAPTER 3

SEVEN PRINCIPLES FOR A CLIMATE INVESTOR

"An investment in knowledge pays the best interest."

— Benjamin Franklin, US founding father

The Climate Investor Framework

To invest successfully in this new era, in the DoE, you must be ready for change. And, while change is the only constant in our shared world, what is also constant is how hard change is for most people. Why? Because when the path is uncharted it can be seen as too fast, too big, and too complex. The fear of the unknown can inspire some, but more often than not, it causes people to slow down or even stop moving forward. That is why I have developed a roadmap; a strategy I call the Seven Principles for a Climate Investor.

Confidence in the legacy of past experience is no longer enough.

So, how do you make smart decisions in what is considered by some to be unproven territory? How do you gain a solid understanding of opportunities and risks so that you can take advantage of them?

You arm yourself with information. You gain a comprehensive understanding of how to make climatech investing work. You learn the new rules of the game, just as investors have done in every previous economic transformation.

You learn and heed this simple climate investment strategy. You learn to heed the Seven Principles for a Climate Investor.

As climate optimists and capitalists, Gigacorn Hunters bring rigorous and creative thought to investing. We look for investments that have the potential to return at least a billion tons of carbon and cross the billion-dollar valuation Rubicon while delivering outstanding profits for investors.

To succeed, I have honed these Seven Principles to find, fund, and grow Gigacorns. By leveraging these principles, you, too, can find opportunities that could become Gigacorns.

You can use them to invest directly or through a fund as a retail, institutional, family office, or as a high-net-worth investor. As a climate entrepreneur, you can use these Principles to understand what climate investors and Gigacorn Hunters need to know so you can refine your investment pitch and help you secure financing. You can also use these principles to cultivate your portfolio.

Now, can you be a climate capitalist without subscribing to all Seven Principles? Yes, but the likelihood of your returns, risk profile and decarbonization of your investments might not perform as well as you anticipated.

Think of it this way: if you bake a cake without sugar or butter, will it look, smell, or taste right? Probably not.

By using the seven principles, you have the foundation to achieve success as a climate investor and a Gigacorn Hunter.

The Seven Principles for a Climate Investor

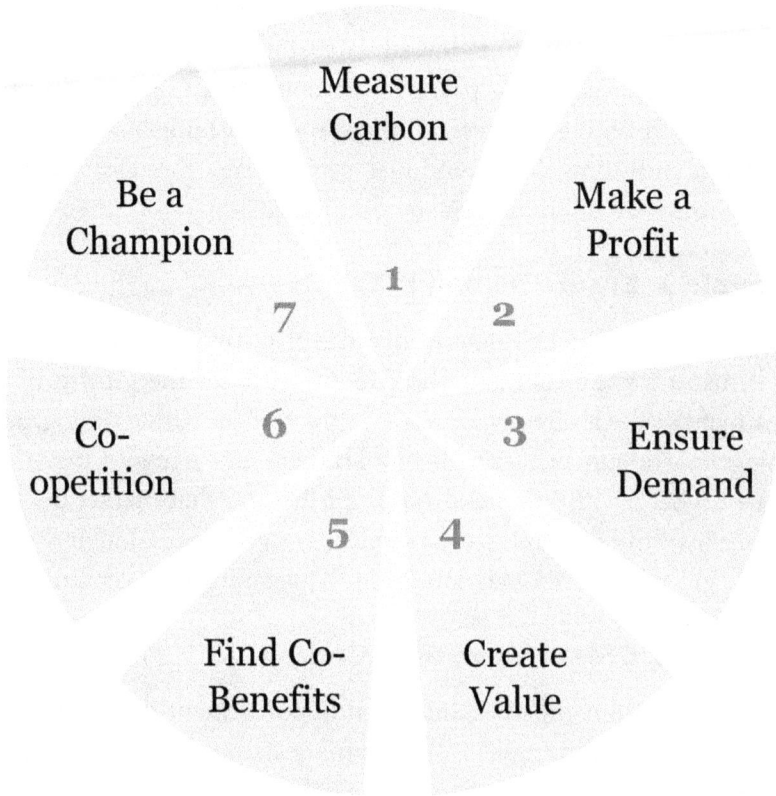

Measure
Carbon

Be a
Champion

Make a
Profit

1

7

2

Co-
opetition

6

3

Ensure
Demand

5

4

Find Co-
Benefits

Create
Value

Principle 1: Measure Carbon

The most exciting Gigacorns will deliver the greatest amount of decarbonization in the shortest period of time. To estimate this and to understand the breadth and scale of an investment's decarbonization potential is fundamental.

You will gain insight into how and how fast the technology delivers decarbonization and how to qualify investments rapidly and measure the investment's potential to deliver real, absolute, and permanent carbon reductions.

Principle 2: Make a Profit

Do not be swayed by the opportunity to deliver exceptional carbon reductions but only middling investment returns. You are not a concessionary investor sacrificing profit for carbon. As a Gigacorn investor, you know that both are necessary to grow and sustain your investment objectives and compel conventional capital into the DoE. Choose investments that will return outstanding profits.

Principle 3: Ensure Demand

The path to successful climatech investment is directly proportional to the demand for the solution. The rate and scale of the growth of the investment's sales is directly related to items such as market timing, positioning and the anchoring proposition. If there is no demand, then there can be no decarbonization and no profit. Ensure that market demand for your investment's products or services is significant enough to drive scalable growth, decarbonization, and follow-on investor demand.

Principle 4: Create Value with Carbon

The best-run run companies understand management governance and how to measure performance. They share decisions with critical stakeholders, including investors, the board, and employees.

They also understand there is always something more to learn that can accelerate growth. This might include creating more value by monetizing the decarbonization an investment delivers or fundamental operational management excellence. You can play an important role by supporting investments with strategic guidance for long-term profitability and decarbonization.

Principle 5: Find Co-benefits

Gigacorn Hunters crave decarbonization and profits. The combination motivates them to dig into an investment. However, there are other benefits that can be delivered through your investment. This might include job creation, water efficiency, enhanced food productivity, energy demand reduction and customer efficiency, among others.

Enumerating these co-benefits help the Gigacorn Hunter with the ultimate investment decision and management guidance once the investment is completed and reveal the benefits beyond carbon, including environmental and social factors, to maximize potential returns and investment impact.

Principle 6: Adopt Co-opetition

Working alone is rarely inspiring. DoE transition investors would be wise to find confederates who bring capital and experience with them to fill gaps to help the investment succeed. Collaborate with other investors and stakeholders—who offer complementary expertise—to accelerate the investment's velocity of value creation and impact.

Principle 7: Be a Champion

Being visible as a climatech and DoE investor tends to recruit more capital, knowledge, and expertise needed to hasten the transition to a low-carbon economy. This includes opportunities to engage with regulators, media, capital providers, entrepreneurs, and more. Your role as a Gigacorn Hunter gives you the opportunity to inspire investors to become Gigacorn Hunters and thus accelerate the transition to the DoE.

Greater Outcomes

By following these Seven Principles, you will find greater confidence in your ability to identify investments with superior profits. You can create sustained returns for your clients, companies and organizations–as well as yourself.

More important, you will invest in businesses with the capacity to restore our planet and sustain communities. You gain satisfaction and pride knowing your investments contribute to a more prosperous future for your children, grandchildren and the generations yet to come.

The first step to climate investing is learning to measure carbon.

Measure the investment's potential to deliver **real, absolute,** and **permanent** *carbon reductions.*

CHAPTER 4

PRINCIPLE 1

MEASURE CARBON

"Measure what is measurable and make measurable what is not so."

— Galileo Galilei, astronomer

My first principle is to measure carbon.

Measure Impact

This conversation took place with my wife, Karen, over the phone, when she was working from home, and I was at the office.

"How long until you are home?" she asked.

"Oh, about fifteen minutes," I replied.

"Great, because I need you to take the kids to the dentist," she said, "and they can't be late."

"No problem," I replied confidently.

Forty minutes later, I arrived home. Traffic turned out to be worse than I had expected. I didn't check Waze to determine the time it might take to get home, as my wife constantly reminds me. My boys had to bear the shame of tartar on their teeth for two more weeks.

It goes to show you how important it is to measure before making decisions.

Measuring Carbon Reduction Potential

To succeed as a climate capitalist, you must maintain carbon performance goals for all your investments, without compromise. By measuring carbon, you determine what your investment can and will deliver in permanent carbon reductions that meet minimum threshold requirements.

That's why my first of the Seven Principles for a Climate Investor is to Measure Carbon: Measure your investment's potential to deliver real, absolute, and permanent carbon reductions.

You will need to quantify how much carbon your investment will need to either avoid emitting and/or remove from the atmosphere. This will improve your understanding of your investment and its true potential.

You don't want to just rely on asking the company how much carbon their solution will eliminate. You need to actually measure it—see, model, and analyze the numbers. You must gauge whether the company goals are realistic and data-driven, or if their promises are pie-in-the-sky wishes—or worse—just plain greenwashing.

If you can't or you don't critically measure carbon, you won't know enough to track progress or maximize the potential climate performance and the return on investment (ROI). It may also fall outside your carbon reduction strategy making it an unfit investment for you.

To validate if a potential investment suits you, focus on three key aspects:

1. Understand the scale, speed and cost of decarbonization;
2. Accurately value the investment; and
3. Know how to engage with the company.

When these three aspects coalesce, you will have achieved the first principle of Gigacorn Hunting. Let's look at the scale, speed and cost of decarbonization. What numbers will excite you enough to invest? How do you know the company's projections are accurate?

The Scale, Speed, and Cost of Decarbonization

Investments in climatech companies will outperform conventional investments in both the medium and long-term, and in many cases, in the short term, as well. Climatech investments will produce better returns than almost all old economy investments where emitting carbon was once considered free and without risk to operations and financial performance, such as coal-fired power generation. This isn't just my opinion. Studies by PwC, BloombergNEF, McKinsey, and the IEA tout the same.[45, 46, 47, 48]

But to see those returns, you need to know the scale, speed, and cost of carbon avoidance or removal. Put another way, how much carbon will be avoided or removed, how fast will the carbon be avoided or removed, and how much will it cost to remove or avoid the carbon? It is essential to know all three in order to qualify whether a potential investment is, in fact, a climatech.

Beginning with the scale, or how much carbon can be avoided or removed, there must be a benchmark to which you can refer. I call this the Minimum Carbon Reduction Potential (mCRP), the amount of carbon a company needs to avoid or remove from the economy. So, the first step is setting your mCRP. My mCRP is '2 by 10': meaning that I need to see at least two tons of carbon avoided or removed for every dollar I have invested into the company within ten years of my initial investment. I sometimes refer to this as 20 by 10 (I need to see at least 20MM tons of carbon avoided or removed within ten years of my initial investment) as I presume that an average investment into a company is $10MM. This threshold has been determined by leaning on a series of key factors including the total mass of carbon that must be removed from the economy, the total cost to deliver this carbon reduction, the proportion of the invested capital that will be wasted on items like duplication of effort and good old-fashioned theft, among other waste, the proportion of the capital needed to unlock the debt that will help finance this transition, a discount factor that is applied to normalize for the scale of risk that climate change poses to the overall economy and society, and the average percent ownership a minority investor holds in a private company. When all these factors are applied the output is 2 tons $CO_2e/\$$ of investment. If a company can demonstrably meet this minimum threshold, it has successfully passed the first hurdle for my consideration.

The speed, how fast the decarbonization will be delivered, or, more specifically, the rate at which the speed of decarbonization will increase, also needs a defined threshold. I call this the Minimum Compound Annual Decarbonization Rate (mCADR). This has proven difficult for many climate investors. But I believe I have developed a solution that is fairly simple—1.5 degrees Celsius, referred to as 1.5C. What does this mean and why did I select it? 1.5C refers to the global average temperature limit the world should stay beneath to avoid the worst impacts of climate change. This is a consensus recommendation of the Nobel Peace Prize winning scientific team of the United Nations Intergovernmental Panel on Climate Change (UN IPCC).[49] If a company can demonstrate that it has a mCADR as fast or faster than the rate of decarbonization needed to meet (or stay below) the 1.5C thresholds, it has successfully passed the second climatech qualification threshold.

The last threshold is the cost, or how much must be spent per ton of carbon avoidance or removal. This is what I call the Minimum Carbon Investment Efficiency (mCIE). Using similar data that is leveraged to determine the mCRP, we can determine what the mCIE should be. The two numbers I rely on first are the estimated cost to achieve decarbonization of the economy by 2050 and the total carbon that must be removed from the economy and the atmosphere. These two numbers are $125 trillion and about 1.2 trillion tons of carbon.[50] When divided, it means the preliminary mCIE is about $100/ton of carbon. When I first conducted this simple calculation, I was amazed because since I can remember, maybe as early as 2005 when I was first involved in government consultations regarding the optimal price of carbon, $100/ton was the magic number, even though we did not yet have any of the data from the UN IPCC or other agencies. The $100/ton number has persisted for twenty years and is sometimes referred to as the Goldilocks Zone for the carbon price, though no one is ever able to answer the question of why $100. Until now. I think it is just a tidy coincidence, but I like when things are tidy.

The story does not end there for the mCIE as, there are a number of other factors I have applied to the $100/ton figure including one for spending efficiency, government policy gaps and factors of safety. Most importantly is a factor that represents the equity portion of the $125 trillion. Why? Because as equity investors, we are interested in the impact of the money we invest. Once these are applied the cost drops precipitously to $5/ton.

Whatever you choose as your minimum thresholds, let each be meaningful enough to help mitigate the fifty billion tons of carbon emitted by the global economy annually and the additional ten billion tons of legacy carbon that remains to be removed from the atmosphere. Then, set each and stick with them. The mCRP, mCADR and mCIE together form the three legs of stool of the first filter in the Gigacorn Hunter's toolkit. Without it, you can't determine if an investment qualifies as a climatech or worth engaging.

Once you have your mCRP, mCADR and mCIE and an interesting investment opportunity, it's time to measure to see the potential of your would-be investment. How much carbon is the investment going to deliver, how fast and at what cost?

I have designed three analytical methods to make these determinations: the Carbon Reduction Potential (CRP), the Compound Annual Decarbonization Rate (CADR) and the Carbon Investment Efficiency (CIE). Look familiar? Each measure is the factor you will calculate and compare against the three legs of the stool, the mCRP, the mCADR and the mCIE.

The CRP is a carbon accounting model rooted in the internationally recognized Greenhouse Gas Protocol (GHG Protocol). It was co-developed by the World Resources Institute and the World Business Council for Sustainable Development.[51] Because the GHG Protocol is used internationally, it's a great way to measure whether a technology aligns with global standards and commonly used calculation methodologies. It helps companies understand their carbon attribution, or how much carbon belongs to them—and how much decarbonization results from their technology.

Wrapping this in as a foundational tool for the CRP model helps you itemize and quantify the various pathways through which decarbonization is delivered over time.

There is yet another factor. It is the Carbon Reduction Intensity (CRI). This is the total decarbonization expected per unit of output of the company through the application of the climatech. Think of it as the number of carbon tons avoided or removed in tons deployed, such as tons per electric vehicle or per carbon capture system.

I find the CRI very useful in rationalizing the CRP and the CIE of the decarbonization. After all, the lower the cost per ton, the more likely the company selling the climatech solution is to succeed. It is also usually the most difficult item to determine. My team and I will often spend a great deal of time researching and consulting experts to find high quality and reliable data to estimate the CRI. It is not only solutions that are first of a kind that require deep analysis. Even proven technologies require technical and statistical analysis to identify and qualify the CRI.

Essentially, the CRP is the product of the CRI and the projected sales of the climatech year over year. As an example, if the company projects to sell ten units in year one, twenty in year two, forty in year three and doubling each year through year ten reaching 5,120 units, with a CRI of 10 tons/unit, then the annual CRPs would be 200 tons, 400 tons and 800 tons reaching 51,200 tons in Year 10. To determine the cumulative CRP over that period, we simply add them together. In this example, the 10-year cumulative CRP is 102,300 tons.

Decarbonization Pathway

Climatech solutions can deliver decarbonization in one or more of three pathways that I call the 3 R's of Decarbonization.

They are:

1. **Reduction**: an increase in the efficiency of an existing solution. For instance, how an LED bulb uses a fraction of the energy of an incandescent bulb.

2. **Replacement**: the wholesale switch from a fossil fuel powered system to a zero-emission alternative. Think of switching from coal-fired power generation to solar power.

3. **Removal**: the physical removal of legacy (previously emitted) anthropogenic (human-induced) carbon emissions. Pulling carbon from the air and permanently storing it.

More succinctly, a reduction pathway slows the rate of carbon emission, while replacement pathways stop emissions, and removal pathways lower atmospheric carbon.

This is all important when conducting your CRP calculation because it helps determine both the ease of conducting the CRP and the net result.

Decarbonization can be delivered directly or indirectly because some climatech solutions directly decarbonize when implemented, as it was made to do.

While indirect technologies don't eliminate carbon emissions, they do make climatech and decarbonization more accessible. Let's say someone develops a new technique that halves the installation cost of solar panels. They didn't actually remove any carbon from the world, but they did remove a roadblock preventing people from accessing solar energy, thus enabling decarbonization.

Knowing whether the decarbonization is delivered directly or indirectly lets you understand how to quantify and qualify the CRP, and how you might encourage additional CRP, as well as how you engage with the company.

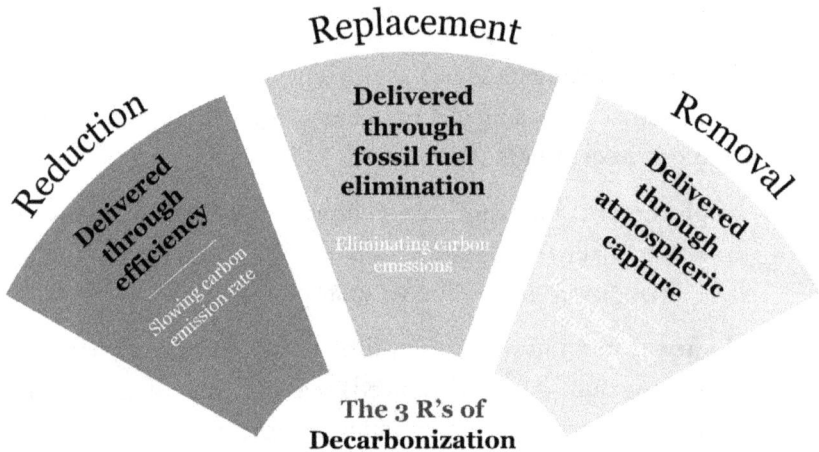

Replacement

Reduction

Delivered through fossil fuel elimination

Removal

Delivered through efficiency

Eliminating carbon emissions

Delivered through atmospheric capture

Slowing carbon emission rate

The 3 R's of
Decarbonization

While the CRP tells you how much carbon the technology will eliminate, it doesn't tell you how fast it might happen. For that, you need the

CADR, which tells you about the rate at which decarbonization occurs over time, or how fast will you see the CRP increase.

For those of you that are familiar with CAGR, the Compound Annual Growth Rate, a commonly used metric in finance, the CADR is essentially the same. It measures the rate of growth of decarbonization and is calculated using the calculated CRP. If we look at the ten-year CRP, the rate of growth represented in percent can be determined over that period. Using the same data as the CRP example above, with year 1 decarbonization of 100 tons and year 10 decarbonization of 51,200 tons, the CADR is 87 percent.

The last leg of the stool, the CIE is a little more unique. It has been designed to help the investor understand how much it costs per unit of carbon removal or avoidance for each dollar of equity invested in the climatech. It is determined using two numbers—the CRP and the total equity invested in the company. Let's look at the same example again. If the total equity invested in the company is projected to be $1MM and the CRP is 102,300 tons then the CIE is $9.78/ton of carbon.

Combined, these numbers (CRP, CADR and CIE) show how much decarbonatization can be delivered, and how swiftly and cost effectively the CRP will grow. It is important to note that these are projections, and, like any financial model, they require a keen eye, discounting and scenario analysis to better ensure confidence in the projections, especially as we are looking at 10-year periods.

Once this modeling and measurement is conducted, this will allow you to understand and the decarbonization and whether it's a good fit for your investment strategy as you compare these numbers to your mCRP, mCADR and mCIE.

CHEAT SHEET

I regret that I must introduce so many acronyms. It is the curse of industry to create and use acronyms that can often confuse those new to a sector. To help bring you into the fold, here's a short glossary of terms:

- **CRP**: *Carbon Reduction Potential.* How much carbon the company's technology may remove from the economy.

- **CADR**: *Compound Annual Decarbonization Rate.* How quickly will the company's rate of decarbonization grow.

- **CIE**: *Carbon Investment Efficiency.* How much it costs to avoid or remove carbon using the company's technology.

- **CRI**: *Carbon Reduction Intensity.* How much carbon is avoided or removed for every unit of the company's technology deployed.

Seeing Decarbonization at Work: LineVision

Electrification of the economy will play an important role in a sustainable low-carbon future. It will reduce the use of fossil fuels in homes, cars, and industries. This means we will need to dramatically increase the electricity grid's capacity to deliver all the electrons required to power our heat pumps, EVs, and manufacturing lines.

Of course, this new capacity must use sustainable and renewable resources like solar, wind, or geothermal. There is an abundance of this renewable capacity just waiting to connect to existing grids, but utilities lack the information they need to bring it online because utilities cannot know how much capacity the grid can truly manage at any given time. This is a function of the legacy systems of our electricity grid.

This demand for more electricity as well as the technological barrier to real time data the utilities are managing had my fund searching for a climatech solution that could increase grid capacity to permit this abundance of renewable power to join the grid with great haste.

Enter LineVision.

Power grids run typically at about 55 percent of capacity because utility operators maintain a large buffer for safety; to try to ensure they do not overload or overheat the lines.[52] If this happens, it can lead to line failure and, in some cases, spark forest fires. LineVision has pioneered a technology called Dynamic Line Rating (DLR), a series of lasers in a box, which bolt on easily to existing transmission towers, and monitor such factors as ambient air temperature, atmospheric pressure, and line sag. This empowers utilities in real-time so they may know how much current can safely pass through the grid at any given point.

LineVision's DLR climatech provides utility operators with the ability to increase grid capacity by as much as 40 percent. This staggering increase provides ample room for renewable energy projects waiting to come online. Between increasing the speed at which renewables can onboard, and decreasing the need to build new transmission lines, LineVision's CRP looked as though it might be impressive to us.

So, we located a climatech capable of marshaling speedy electrification transitions. But, before jumping into a LineVision investment, we researched its CRP.

How much carbon could LineVision reduce, replace, or remove?

We ran the CRP model and began by identifying the pathways through which decarbonization could be delivered. We determined that there are four main pathways: additional renewable capacity coming onto the grid (Direct Reduction and Indirect Replacement); avoided emissions from new transmission lines (direct Reduction); avoided emissions from forest fires (direct Reduction); and acceleration of the electrification of the economy (indirect Reduction and Replacement).

We found data supporting the first three pathways. I like to get my hands into CRP models because there is so much to learn. For instance, it turns out that 80 percent of the electricity production capacity waiting to come online in the United States is renewable.[53] It is also amazing that forest fires are the single largest source of carbon emissions in California where 35 percent of those fires are caused by failed power lines, according to National Public Radio.[54]

For the fourth pathway, given the level of difficulty in calculating the impact of LineVision on the electrification of the overall economy, which was quite complex, we noted it, but we did not model it. If a pathway proves too difficult to model, it has been my experience that it is usually because the decarbonization is too indirect and likely only nominally attributable to your climatech. This is not a rule, and honest effort should be made to examine it, but it is a good piece of guidance to consider.

Not modeling the fourth pathway hardly mattered as the CRP, once calculated, netted over 50 million tons of carbon within the first 10 years of our investment period. This significantly exceeded the mCRP.

The CADR and the CIE proved to be equally compelling, outstripping the mCADR and mCIE by wide margins. Visions of a Gigacorn danced in my head.

With numbers like these followed by very supportive diligence findings, investing in LineVision was a no-brainer. Our team moved quickly assembling a syndication of investors that included Microsoft's Climate Fund, S2G Ventures, and Marubeni Corp. They saw what we saw.

DON'T DRIVE WITHOUT FIRST LOOKING UNDER THE HOOD

We are often drawn to Gigacorn hunting because we are passionate about solving climate challenges. Companies that want our investments know that, and they adjust course to sell into it. Investors need to remove their rose-colored glasses and be hard-nosed and realistic. Don't just take the investment's carbon reduction or life cycle assessment models at face value. Do your own research, calculate your CRP, your CADR and your CIE, and make sure this investment meets or exceeds your minimums.

What valuation did we assign to LineVision in our term sheet? And how did we know what the right amount was? The next thing you need to learn is how to use your model, the tool you use to calculate your CRP, CADR and CIE, to enhance your ability to appropriately value an investment.

There is a terrific quote from Professor George Box, a famous statistician who taught at the University of Wisconsin-Madison who once said, "All models are wrong, but some models are useful."[55]

This is a perfect example of that principle. Even if your model is wrong, and it is bound to be given the ten-year projections and all the dependent factors and variables used to conduct the calculations, it is very helpful at guiding decisions, including the valuation decision.

Appropriately Value Your Investments

The more disruptive the technology, the higher its valuation will likely be, and the better the ROI. When you understand how the company decarbonization will be delivered, and how much, and how soon that will be, and at what cost, the more effectively you can price the deal.

The exit valuation is, after all, how you as an investor make your money and become a true climate capitalist.

That's why understanding how to appropriately value potential investments before you commit is fundamental to the principles of being an effective and profitable Gigacorn Hunter.

You will often find yourself competing for deals. If you see a good one, chances are others will, too. Imagine that someone submits a term sheet and says they value the company at $100 million, and they want you to invest $10 million. Somebody else might say, "We value the company at $150 million, and we're going to give you $10 million." Who's right?

The correct answer can be found in the math.

COMPANY VALUATIONS FACTORS

Before investing, a savvy VC undertakes rigorous modeling of a company. They consider factors including but not limited to:

- How disruptive the value proposition is
- Sales traction and pipeline (i.e. customers)
- Market size and demand
- Revenue and revenue model
- Competition and differentiation
- Merger & Acquisition market
- Technology protection and barriers to entry
- Executive team

By reflecting some combination of these factors in a financial model, investors usually end up with a reasonable company valuation.

But something important is missing from this financial model: the three legs of our carbon stool, the CRP, CADR and CIE.

Gigacorn Hunters who incorporate the details behind the carbon model into the financial model often feel more confident assigning a valuation that is higher than their more traditional counterparts. Understanding the CRP's pathways, scale, speed and cost can also help identify the carbon monetization potential. This will translate into a carbon valuation premium, which can range from minor to significant. I have seen these premiums range from zero to more than 25 percent.

When my investment team uncovers a good decarbonization story, an entrepreneur who has developed a technology capable of generating revenue and reputational benefit directly associated with the carbon being avoided or removed that is above and beyond the financial model and projections provided to us, we have a competitive advantage in the case of a bidding war. Our knowledge of the climate and carbon landscapes paired with the carbon modeling we conducted gives us an edge. It positions us to lead the deal and secure a seat at the boardroom table.

The opposite has played out, too. Investors who simply take an entrepreneur's word for it when it comes to the decarbonization, it's scale and monetization potential. I am yet to see an entrepreneur who did not attribute too much decarbonization to their technology the same way every company seems to overstate their revenue projections. When this happens, investors may find themselves overpaying for an investment. These are the types of deals where I typically lean out.

Do the math. Always do the math.

The Widget That Didn't

A venture fund I had collaborated with previously contacted me proclaiming, "We've got this really cool technology we are going to invest in. You're going to love it! It's going to trigger a residential solar adoption explosion." It turned out they wanted to invest in a company that had developed a widget that allows you to integrate residential solar power more easily. It would reduce the cost of a typical solar panel installation from $25,000 to $24,000.

They predicted they would deliver at least 100 million tons of carbon within five years. That sounded incredibly impressive—but was it true?

They were kind enough to share their carbon calculation with us, and when I dug in, it became clear that their math had several fatal flaws. For instance, when the venture fund calculated the company's decarbonization potential, they attributed all the reductions from installing and operating a solar panel on a person's roof to their widget. That was wildly inaccurate and violated the GHG Protocol principal of share of ownership. At best, they could claim only 1/24th of the reduction, since they were lowering the installation price by $1000 or 1/24th.

They also presumed the carbon intensity of the grid would not change over the widget's lifetime. Knowing that over 80 percent of new power generation coming onto the grid is renewable, then the carbon factor would be discounted. Add that to their assumption that this widget was projected to be adopted in 70 percent of all residential solar installations, and you have a cascading waterfall leading to a massive overestimation of the CRP.

We took a pass on the deal and advised the fund that brought it to us to do the same.

Engage the Company

Part of your role as a Gigacorn Hunter is to advise the companies and entrepreneurs in which you invest. Thanks to your previous carbon modeling work, you understand decarbonization expectations, how it is delivered, and how that impacts company value. You can bring those insights to bear when you advise the management team. That's valuable to both of you—so long as they respect your expertise.

To get the most as both an investor and an advisor, you must establish a healthy and ongoing relationship with management throughout the deal process, so that when you close the deal and attend your first board meeting, you are welcomed. To help this along, you need to manage expectations. You can better ensure this if you include specific language into your term sheet and final deal documents. Contract language can be an effective tool both to lay bare expectations and to hold people accountable.

Antonella Penta, my friend and corporate lawyer, with decades of deal experience, has counseled me on this several times, "As a deal lawyer, nothing's worse than when a dispute arises, and people turn to the contract for resolution. It's terrifying—'Did I miss something? Was I clear enough? Could I have done more?' That's why we draft agreements as if they'll be scrutinized in court. Ambiguity is a lawyer's worst enemy."

Antonella even reminded me of Justice Scalia's words: "The main business of a lawyer is to take the romance, the mystery, the irony, the ambiguity out of everything he touches." It's Antonella's philosophy too, and one that's served me well ever since. It will do the same for you.

Whenever possible, I insert in my deal terms or term sheets requirements for the investees to measure and report their carbon performance. They need to forecast their CRP, track progress, and provide reports to the board. At least once per quarter, we review the numbers to see how they did. Did they underperform, overperform, or hit the nail on the carbon head? That helps our team monitor the investment's health, and it often opens the door to productive discussions around strategy and tactics that can enhance performance and ultimate returns.

> ## SAMPLE CONDITIONS FOR DEAL DOCUMENT
>
> Here are some examples of wording to consider inserting into your term sheets. What you include and how these terms are crafted depends entirely on how the carbon reductions or removals are delivered:
>
> 1. **For all investments**: Not later than one hundred and eighty (180) days following the Closing, the Company will report to the board, using an accepted methodology, an estimation of the total carbon sequestered by the Company to date and update the report every three (3) months to report estimated net new carbon avoided or removed since the prior reporting period.
>
> 2. **For investments where the carbon monetization pathways are clear**: Within ninety (90) days after the Closing, the Company will retain qualified internal and/or external resources required to deliver a Carbon Strategy acceptable to the fund (acting reasonably), including, but not limited to, reporting protocols, the development plan for certified carbon credits, and a carbon monetization plan.

Ensuring the terms and conditions include carbon accounting and reporting requirements allows you to maintain insights into both decarbonization and value creation opportunities.

It also allows us to identify and work closely with a company on opportunities to create more value. With your additional information and area of expertise, you bring value to the table. The company's C-suite wants to work with you as much as you want to work with them. They will also often favor you as the lead investor, because you engage with them in ways that others might not be able to match.

Using Your Calculations for the Company's Good

Thanks to this new insight, you may understand a company's capabilities even better than they do. That was the case for one of our investments.

I was approached by a start-up called Manifest Climate with an invitation to invest. It is a Software as a Service platform that allows users, usually large corporations and asset managers, to understand how conformant they are with carbon risk regulations and standards, such as the Task Force for Climate-Related Financial Disclosure. With the insights gained through the Manifest platform, managers and the boards to whom they report can make better climate risk management decisions.

Research shows that people who manage and disclose their climate risk decarbonize at a faster rate than those who do not disclose their carbon risk.[56] So, I knew that their software could result in significant decarbonization, but how could I calculate just how much? Like most companies, Manifest Climate had no internal system for calculating their CRP.

I wondered: if Manifest Climate has a tool that enables companies to decarbonize, how much of that company's decarbonization can we claim it helped to deliver?

My team researched and determined the difference between companies that disclose their climate risk and those that do not, from a percentage rate of decarbonization. We then divided companies into large corporations, enterprise-level, and mid-market companies. From there, we organized them by industry, a company in mining versus one in finance, for instance, differed significantly with or without disclosure.

We came up with impressive, data-derived numbers. There was still an element of assumption—there had to be—but we felt reasonably confident that within ten years, based on the customers Manifest Climate was targeting, it would be responsible for between 20 and 30 million tons of carbon being avoided or removed. Seeing the value-add that our company, ClimateIC, brought to the table, they were eager to bring us on.

**TIP FOR NEWLY MINTED GIGACORN HUNTERS
(AND VETERANS ALIKE)**

When you set out to pick your first investments, don't fall for a low CRP in exchange for high profit. Equally, don't fall for high CRP with low profit. An effective climate capitalist looks for companies that hit both. They know their minimums and thresholds, and they stick to that framework.

As my father, a civil engineer and builder, told me on more than one occasion, measure twice and cut once. Once you have measured and found that an investment opportunity fits your criteria for carbon, the next criteria to check is whether it can actually make a profit.

Choose **investments** that will **return** **outstanding** *profits.*

CHAPTER 5

PRINCIPLE 2

MAKE A PROFIT

"The wealth being generated in climate tech right now will wildly eclipse all of the wealth ever generated by the Internet total."

— Chris Sacca, Venture Investor

Can You Predict a Great Return?

Imagine that it's June 28, 2010 (my mother's birthday, as it turns out). Your friend calls you about a great new investment opportunity. He tells you about a startup called Tesla, and he tells you they make electric cars.

"Electric cars?" you ask. "Is there a market for that?"

You do some research, and it seems like the road to production and market adoption is filled with sharp curves and sudden drop-offs. There is significant risk.

But this a trusted friend you're talking with. If the founder—some guy named Musk—can get an electric vehicle to work, it'll be a major game changer. You have a chance here to get in on the ground floor of something potentially huge. But there is a great deal of risk involved, so you decide to play it safe and invest only $1,000, and then you'll wait see.

Fast forward thirteen years to 2023. Tesla is a leading manufacturer of EVs, selling two million of them, up about 40 percent from its prior year. Your $1,000 stock investment is now worth $220,000. That's a 21,000 percent ROI. You made ten times more than the return on Apple, Amazon, or any other stock over the same period. You could have made more, if you had been more confident about the road ahead for Tesla back in 2010 and been following on with additional investment along the way.

Looking back, it seems obvious that you should have invested more, but in the moment, there were so many questions circling Tesla—the technology, demand, the infrastructure, and the likely competition from the world's most successful automobile brands and other new would-be EV companies. What could you have done to invest more confidently? How could you have predicted which companies would deliver the biggest returns and which would hit the wall?

Make a Profit, Don't Be Just Profitable

Your decision of 2010 may seem obvious today, but it bears saying, especially for climate capitalists: For an investment to succeed, it must provide an ROI. That means the value of the company, or at least your investment in it, must increase.

Principle 2 of my Seven Principles for a Climate Investor is: Make a Profit: Choose investments that will return outstanding profits.

The more profitable the Gigacorn is for its investors, the more capital will flow into the DoE and the faster the transition to a low carbon economy will occur.

Providing capital to a company and not expecting a return is philanthropy. While many organizations and people make donations, and we should all donate where and when we can to charities in which we believe, it is not a sustainable investment model.

That is why your focus must be on making profits. The greater your profits, the more you will be able to donate to not-for-profits.

As a Gigacorn Hunter, you should always keep in mind these three fundamental aspects:

1. Know what drives investment returns;
2. Help compel conventional investors; and
3. Understand your fiduciary responsibilities.

There is a distinction between an investment being profitable and an investment returning profits to investors. You may be familiar with the idea of an investment that becomes EBITDA (earnings before interest, taxes, depreciation, and amortization) positive. Many investors want a company to spit out loads of cash in the form of dividends—they want it to be profitable. That is certainly desirable, but it's only one way to think about investment returns.

Gigacorn Hunters want a company to increase in value over time. They want to make profits for investors. That is different from a company being profitable. This principle is about ensuring you have the evidence you need to feel confident that an investment is going to provide substantial returns to you in the form of overall valuation before you exit.

Making a profit is about intellectual muscle, not emotional muscle. Ethics should be part of your math, but they cannot drive your investment decisions. When you know how to prove an investment will make a profit above and beyond the returns of the conventional economy (think oil and gas), you can demonstrate it is better to invest in climatech than in traditional sectors. By doing so, you will accelerate the pace of the DoE era as a whole. You help the transition of climatech investments from perceived, or qualitative, value creation to the quantitative.

If there is one thing I have learned over my years in business and investing, it is to invest with your brain, rather than your heart.

Ignore this second of the Seven Principles at your peril. You can't invest in companies based solely on what you think will do the most good for the planet. If you do this right, you will save the planet because you invest with your head.

I have watched people invest in companies because they think it's the right thing to do. They make choices with lofty ambitions but poor returns...and then they lose everything. I made that mistake several times in the early 2000s and I have no intention of repeating it: Finavera Renewables is one of those lessons. I remember making the decision to invest in a predecessor of this renewable energy developer that was acquired by Finervera because I wanted to support the growth of renewables. After all, I wanted to see wind power replace fossil fuels. The company was publicly traded on the Toronto Stock Exchange, had wind power projects in British Colombia and Ireland, a partnership with GE Power, and a compelling wave technology, too. Fast forward a few years and the stock floundered as it lost or sold assets and projects and renamed itself several times.[57] I eventually lost track of its whereabouts after it disappeared altogether from my trading portfolio.

If you invest solely with your heart, your wants, then you will most likely misallocate capital and your investments will deliver suboptimal returns, or even losses, hurting more than just your bottom line.

Moreover, if you make investments that fail, those who are dedicated to the good old days, to maintaining the status quo that is the environmentally and socially destructive conventional economy, may point to you as an example of why people should not invest in the DoE. After all, they largely believe it is in their interest to slow and stop the advancement of climatech and sustainable finance.

To make a profit, as often as possible, you must know which companies to bet on. Then, you must compel conventional investors to join you in supporting and championing them. Finally, if you are a fund manager, you should uphold your responsibility to your fund investors, and steadfastly act in their best interests.

Your goal should be to make the best-informed, pragmatic decisions in the pursuit of your mandate to deliver outsized financial returns while simultaneously delivering the greatest amount of decarbonization in the shortest period of time.

So, how do you increase the likelihood that you will make money?

Know What Drives Returns

Obviously, you intend to invest in companies that will make money and provide superior returns. That may be obvious in traditional investing, but in climate investing, many people like to think of themselves as ethical investors willing to take suboptimal returns to help bring climatech innovation to life. It's a point worth hammering home. Climate investors are non-concessionary. We do not give up returns for the sake of climate impact. As I have shared numerous times before, we do not need to. And, for the DoE to be successful, the climatech on which we will rely must be sustainable, economically as well and environmentally and socially. They must deliver returns that ensure they can sustain themselves. Do not fall into the trap of mistaking investing for philanthropy.

Philanthropy does not make money. Say it with me, "*Philanthropy does not make money.*"

Investing in not-for-profit activities may be commendable, but it should be conducted outside of a returns-based fund mandate. Your goal should be to grow capital, which means before you make an investment, you must ensure the return on capital and internal rate of return can be determined using traditional, fundamental financial analysis such as performance forecasting, cash flow, demand, valuation, and entrance and exit multiple analysis.

If you do that, you will choose opportunities that are more likely to deliver the return you want.

If you're a professional fund manager, you already know and use all of this, but, if you aren't, then work with someone who is, so they can help you navigate this landscape, which will be familiar to them even if they aren't climatech investors. All they're doing is extending their critical criteria into a new investing segment. I'll discuss this more in Chapter 6, when I discuss how to create value for the companies in which you invest.

ENVIRONMENTAL, SOCIAL, AND GOVERNANCE (ESG)

Some investors use environmental, social, and governance (ESG) data to help them decide if a startup will be a good investment. This is often misunderstood as an investment philosophy, but ESG is a series of data points that can be used to enhance your investment decision-making.

Sandra Odendahl, Senior Vice President and Head, Sustainability, Diversity & Social Impact with the Business Development Bank of Canada puts it this way:

"ESG isn't an agenda; it's a way to ensure that financially material environmental, social and governance issues are considered alongside traditional financial measures, when valuing securities or making an investment decision. The more you know, the better you can navigate risks, and make smart, profitable decisions. Unfortunately, people have been using "ESG" to mean 100 different things, and it's no surprise that this has created problems."

I've known and worked with Sandra for nearly 20 years and have always found she has a way of cutting through the noise. ESG, when understood correctly, is simply a value-added tool that enhances decision-making, not some philosophical stance.

In the US, some state governments have created anti-ESG measures, refusing to invest state funds with asset managers that use ESG data to make decisions. The controversy stems largely from a misunderstanding about what ESG is and that it may pose a risk to the conventional economy, such as oil and gas sectors, and the jobs in districts these politicians represent.

They seem to me to misunderstand what ESG is, even though the definition is quite simple: It's just a framework for gathering all the material data. Using ESG doesn't make you inherently pro- or anti-environment. It just makes you a more informed investor and decision-maker.

Refusing to invest with an asset manager who uses ESG is folly, or so it seems to me. Basing your investment decisions solely on ESG data doesn't help you know if an investment will produce profits, but incorporating ESG into the investment research, and analysis process will help you understand the broader material risks and opportunities. If you aspire to be a savvy Gigacorn Hunter, I advise you to use ESG hand-in-hand with your traditional financial tools.

Good PR, Bad Business

It goes wrong fast when you don't apply a financial framework to your climate investing. I saw it happen when I was working at Nestlé Waters in 2016. As Chief Sustainability Officer, while on a stakeholder engagement tour in New York, I was approached by students who had developed an app to incentivize recycling. They wanted to put a QR code on every campus recycling receptacle. Users would scan the code, and then the UPC code of whatever they were depositing, to earn points they could exchange for rewards.

I arranged for them to present to my team. The presentation was dramatic, passionate, and rational. Shortly after the students finished, they thanked us for listening and departed. My team quickly recommended against investing. Quantitatively, their proposal required a very high level of engagement and effort by end users—and there was no model for sustainable revenue beyond seeking donations from companies like Nestlé. Encouraged to conduct some quantitative work, my team completed some analysis, which indicated there would be no positive return on the invested capital for Nestlé or the students and therefore it would not become financially sustainable. It was philanthropy.

Our marketing team saw it differently. They thought it presented a great PR opportunity. So, they presented it to my colleague, the Chief Marketing Officer. He and the team thought it was a great opportunity. The students had used qualitative arguments in lieu of quantitative ones: it would engage the campus population, enhance the sustainability credibility of those involved with the platform, and could eventually be rolled out to other universities.

Our marketing team invested. I think it would be fairer to characterize it as a sponsorship, but the money had been raised by these students with promise of a return.

As predicted, the app failed. The company wasn't capitalized appropriately and had under-advertised. Most important, the company's research indicated the system was too cumbersome.

Show me a student who wants to stand at a trash bin, scan it, then scan each piece of recyclable trash before depositing it. Then they would go into the app to check how many points they've earned, and after all that, they would check the rewards list to see if they had qualified for or any reward they wanted.

This investment failed because the students put their hearts in front of their heads in what was intended to be a for-profit enterprise. They wanted to demonstrate sustainability, and they thought students would engage because they're environmentally aware. But you can't qualify an investment based on intuition. Just like any other investment, you must look at your demand analysis, customer segmentation, your technology, and so on.

If you're building an investment memo for a climatech investment, make sure you include both quantitative and qualitative arguments. You can and should be able to marry sustainability criteria with conventional criteria. It's the best way to increase the likelihood you will make a profit—and attract conventional investors.

Compel Conventional Investors

Since 2006, the proportion of total private capital invested in climatech has increased from 1.4 percent to over 11.4 percent, according to CB Insights, a market intelligence and analytics service for investors.[58] This massive increase isn't being driven by philanthropists or even Gigacorn Hunters, but by the simple facts of performance and promise.

Climatech is a good investment. For traditional investors, that's what matters most.

Conventional investors are generally agnostic about what they invest in. They're not evil or amoral; they just have a profit priority. As long as the likelihood and scale of the potential return meet their threshold, they will want in. They control the lion's share of all investible capital. That's why it is so important to compel conventional investors to join us in the DoE.

Bringing their capital to climatech deployment has a two-fold impact:

1. It accelerates the growth of climatech, and therefore decarbonization; and
2. It removes capital from carbon-intensive sectors such as oil and gas, which further accelerates decarbonization.

Engaging conventional investors is all about showing them that there are exceptional opportunities that deliver not just good returns but better returns than in the conventional economy and with more attractive risk profiles.

New climatech investors often remember earlier days, when returns were poor or non-existent. Decisions were largely being made based on the ability of technology to solve an environmental problem rather than a business problem. They wondered, if this is true, what changed? When did the returns start to take off?

There was no single world-changing moment, but a continuing series of modest events. As local, national, and international policy came into force, corporate and asset manager commitments expanded and climatech innovations began to consistently and reliably outperform conventional solutions.

The demand for solutions has grown exponentially. Layering on top of this, the physical manifestations of climate-impacting incidents such as forest fires across every inhabited continent, and the increased frequency and volatility of floods and droughts, no one can deny the reality of climate change. That has led to capital being deployed to expand renewable power and other climatech activities.

Investors are taking note of this market shift. For example, Larry Fink is chairman, CEO and co-founder of Blackrock. With $10 trillion in assets under management, Blackrock is the world's largest global investment group.[59]

In his 2022 annual letter to CEOs, Fink recommended everyone to shift into renewable energy investments. He told CEOs worldwide, that the next 1,000 unicorns will be green energy companies, and predicted that, "The unicorns are coming!" He went on to predict, "Every company and every industry will be transformed by the transition to a net zero world. The question is, will you lead, or will you be led."[60]

His point is simple: when there's transformation and disruption in the marketplace, there's money to be made. So, there's not a moment to lose! Get in there!

THE LIGHTBULB STANDARD

If you want proof that climate technology is rising, look no further than the humble lightbulb. When LED lightbulbs first came out, the upfront purchase price was about three times that of a similar incandescent bulb. Of course, they lasted almost twenty years and cut electricity costs that whole time. Still, the initial cost was an investment in future savings.

Not so anymore. By 2023, an LED lightbulb cost less than a traditional incandescent bulb, and as the number of such climatech examples continue to mount, the argument to compel conventional investors is becoming increasingly easier.

Fulfill Your Fiduciary Responsibility

As an asset manager, you are bound by your fiduciary responsibility to act in the best interests of your clients. This ensures trust, safeguards investors, and promotes ethical conduct.

As a Gigacorn Hunter, your responsibility includes the environmental and social implications of decision-making as well as the financial issues. I would argue this is true for all investors; a debate that has been going on at least since 2005.

It has been led by Paul Watchman, a pioneering sustainability finance lawyer and academician who has made significant contributions to environmental, social, and governance (ESG) investing, climate change law, and human rights in business. I had the pleasure of meeting and engaging with Paul in 2005 when he released a landmark report known as the Freshfields Report arguing that failing to incorporate environmental and social factors in investment decision-making was a breach of fiduciary duty.[61]

For as long as I can remember, issues like climate, water, and social risk have been considered externalities, meaning they were outside the scope of fiduciary responsibility. The conduct of a business may result in any combination of these factors being compromised in some way, but existing legislation meant the company would not bear the financial burden of reversing these impacts. Usually, the public and taxpayers end up paying for these factors. As such, the prevailing argument was that these risks did not pose a material risk to corporate financial performance. Some even argued that this meant that focusing on environmental issues, either their prevention or clean-up, would breach fiduciary responsibility given the added cost the offending company may bear.

We knew better then. Now, we all know better.

These factors have a deep material impact on financial performance, and so, if you are an asset manager, and you have promised to act in the best interests of your clients, you must consider ESG issues, climate foremost among them, perhaps. Understanding and assessing these factors not only to protect from loss, but to maximize gains. As a Gigacorn Hunter, you should understand this better than others.

A Financial Risk Is a Poor Investment

I've put this into practice many times.

Many years ago, I advised an energy company that wanted to invest in power generation assets to hedge its retail electricity business through vertical integration. They were considering investing in coal power stations, and they wanted my advice. Well, to be clear, I learned of the pending transaction and insisted I be given the chance to assess the opportunity using an ESG lens.

I did the math and presented them with a one-page report. It included one chart. It indicated that in the first two years, the company would make lots of money burning coal and selling electrons. But as new carbon, air quality and health regulations came into play, the cost of coal power would rise, and profits would decline. As the cost of carbon continued to rise, it would become a liability.

The climate transition risk posed to the business by virtue of carbon regulation, was the primary driver of the simple model I provided, but there were other significant factors, including potential litigation from communities suffering negative health outcomes from the industrial pollution.

I'm pleased to say the company passed on the investment. It was not only because of the scope of the climate risk, but it played a part. Integrating ESG into this investment decision enhanced the company's ability to make a financially responsible decision because they now better understood the risk.

This has been playing out in public markets spectacularly in recent years. In 2020, BP, Royal Dutch Shell, and other oil and gas supermajors wrote down the value of their oil and gas reserves by nearly $40 billion.[62] The impact of climate risk meant that reserves they once considered as valuable assets were now unlikely to be developed.

When you calculate what makes money, convince others to join you in investing, and protect the assets of those who trust you with their money, you are ready to make a profit. But first, you must ensure the market demands the technology you're considering.

I'll tell you more about that in the next chapter.

Ensure that *market demand* for the **investment's products or services** are **sufficiently significant** to **drive growth, decarbonization,** and follow-on investor demand.

CHAPTER 6

PRINCIPLE 3

ENSURE DEMAND

"Nothing happens until a sale is made."

— Thomas Watson, first IBM CEO

The Push to Purchase

Consider how many times you heard about a new environmentally friendly product and thought, "Wow, I'm going to try that!" Perhaps a friend recommended it, and you thought it sounded like a great alternative that would prevent environmental impacts.

But the real test comes when you, the shopper, are standing in the aisle of a popular store and you see the new green product right next to the product you have been using for years. Your hand drifts over to that old, familiar standby—the one you have used for years.

Maybe you don't believe the new offering will work as well or it costs a little more. Perhaps you don't have any pressing need to stop buying what you have always bought.

Welcome to the say-do paradox. The term refers to the discrepancy between what people say they will do and what they will end up doing.

It highlights the inconsistency often observed between stated intentions and actual behavior.

It is a common phenomenon in consumer behavior, environmental actions, and personal commitments. As in the example above, in consumer behavior, individuals may express strong intentions to purchase an eco-friendly product but then they opt for their familiar old standbys when making actual purchases. They change their minds due to factors like price, convenience, or availability, or, most commonly, habit.

It is a bigger issue than just purchase decisions. We often renege on promises we make to ourselves. For example, you may have vowed to exercise regularly but then fail to adhere to this routine due to a lack of motivation or time, or an inability to break your daily routine.

My point is that most people aren't willing to change their buying habits until there is an acknowledgment or problem that a new solution can solve or solve better than the product you have used for years.

To be confident that a new product has real market potential, you must understand exactly what will cause demand.

Can You Find the Demand?

Before you invest, confirm that there is sufficient demand for the offering these entrepreneurs have developed. Determine that demand from customers and other investors is so significant that the new solution will not only disrupt conventional buying, but it will also drive significant decarbonization and attract follow-on investment.

Without the ability to accurately gauge market demand, your investment is likely to underperform in both revenue and CRP, meaning the value of the investment will fall. Not only will you not meet your investment return goals, but you will also lose capital. The investment will likely also struggle to raise capital in subsequent rounds, which will lead to cash flow issues. You will be hard-pressed to realize a successful exit, and you definitely won't be able to take advantage of the ROI by redeploying that capital into a new investment opportunity.

The three fundamentals to Ensuring Demand are:

1. The customer always matters;
2. Demand is independent of regulation; and
3. Establish a competitive advantage.

When you follow these fundamentals, you can better predict how the revenues coming from the company's products or services will grow. If not, you will likely be pouring money in to subsidize operations due to shortfalls in cash from lack of revenue. Of course, some businesses have succeeded, because investors kept pumping money in until the company found its path to profitability. That was the case with Amazon and Uber, and investors did exceptionally well.

The difference between that and failing to ensure demand is that Amazon was always able to demonstrate continued growth, hyperbolic growth. When that happens, you gain some runway to reach profitability. But at the end of the day, that just buys time—if the customers don't come, neither do the profits for the company or your investment portfolio.

ARE YOU ALL-IN?

Ensuring demand is important. If you don't, you could see your invested capital drop to zero, hampering your ability to invest in your next opportunity, one which might have brighter and more lucrative prospects.

Customers Matter

Nothing matters more to the success of your investment than the willingness of a critical mass of customers to adopt and stick with your investment's product or service—nothing.

Understanding the business's challenges and how the solution meets those challenges is vital. It leads to revenue, which drives growth potential. The good news is that maintaining strong relationships with customers doesn't just help you as an investor: It also helps the company in the long-term by creating a funnel for valuable feedback to drive innovation, enhancements to products, and referrals, all of which drive growth.

If you don't have a marketing background, understanding what drives customers can be tricky. Even professional marketers would volunteer that it is tricky for them. I'm always struck by the say-do paradox I have described above—the delta between what customers say they'll buy, and what they actually will buy. Knowing whether this delta is positive or negative, and to what degree, is critical to knowing if the customer will help drive you to your investment goals.

This paradox is the main reason behind the failure of Cleantech 1.0. Cleantech 1.0 represented the first wave of clean technology innovation and investment that occurred between about 2006 and 2011. It produced a surge of $25 billion in venture capital investment and focused on technologies like solar energy, biofuels, smart grids, and energy efficiency, among others.[63]

Cleantech 1.0 faced many challenges, such as high capital intensity, long development cycles and scaling barriers.

Cleantech 1.0 is often referred to as a VC failure. Nearly half the $25 billion invested was lost or impaired, and more than 90 percent of the cleantech companies funded failed to return even the initial capital invested.[64]

Cleantech 1.0 did succeed in generating a tremendous number of technologies capable of solving incredibly challenging environmental and social issues. However, most of these solutions did not to solve a business issue or a customer problem (Remember Enphase from the Introduction). Customers buy when you solve a problem they are facing, or, in some cases, when your solution can expand areas of opportunity. Since these environmental and social innovations did not solve a problem businesses considered material to them (rightly or wrongly), there was no real buy-in or market demand.

That changed after the Paris Agreement. Suddenly, there was demand stimulated from a combination of recognition of the science, mandates and commitments across industries. Finally, customers were calling. The inflection caused demand to cross the critical line for solutions.

Demand for climatech solutions now exceeds the level of investment

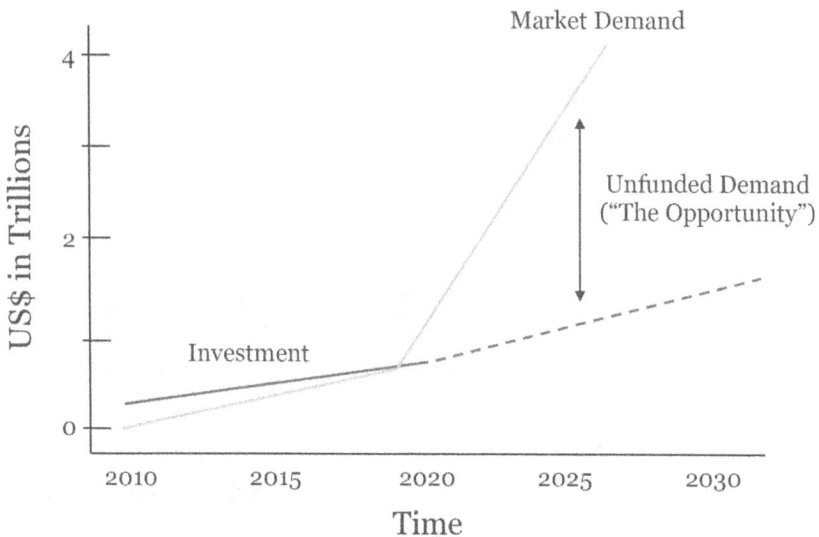

Before making any investment, it is critical to engage in conversations with customer prospects. Nothing reduces the risk from investment decisions better than speaking with users. Of course, this is easier to do when the product or service is already on the market, but you can also speak with potential clients and gauge whether the delta of the say-do paradox has been closed.

When speaking to customers, ask questions like:

- What will the product or service be used for? What challenge does it solve?
- How many times have they bought it?
- What benefits are they reaping?
- Have they ever recommended the product to a colleague, friend, or family member?
- What stops them from switching to another product?
- What motivates them to switch to a new product?

The answers will let you know if your potential investment has a fighting chance. If it does, then it will lead to revenue, which drives growth potential. The more you understand the demand side from the customer, the more you can gauge whether or not your potential investment understands the customer. If not, they will never find real success.

ALL CUSTOMERS ARE NOT CREATED EQUAL

When you look for customers to talk with, especially if the investment is a business-to-business (B2B) company, make sure you're speaking to qualified buyers who will be signing the check— not just the enthusiastic junior team members. So often, I see lower-level management fall in love with a solution, but then they fail to get approval to transition the company over, to buy.

Of course, there are times when customers don't know if they need a particular product or service. In such cases, the business will likely be focused on education. Gauge their strategy to get an idea of how they plan to reach new customers and why they think they'll be able to educate them on the service. Do they have a drafting strategy (following competitors)? Do they know how they plan to replace existing providers? Is there a specific, identifiable customer problem that the company can solve? If they can demonstrate need, it's a good indication that demand exists.

Be wary, however, if the entrepreneur espouses the phrase, "We are creating a new category!" Creating a new category is typically very difficult, very costly, and takes quite a long time. My partner Kevin at ClimateIC often says, "You only know that you have created a new category after you've actually done it." So, if the company founder is convinced they have created a new category before the company has sold product, you may have identified an investment to avoid.

So again, be mindful of category creators.

Two Ways to Ensure Demand

When you conduct due diligence, you must ensure demand on two fronts: buyers and investors. You must determine if the investment's product or service is needed by a critical mass of customers who will indeed buy the product, and also that they can raise sufficient capital to execute and grow the business.

These two elements are connected. The greater the market demand, the higher the likelihood other investors will want to invest—or buy the company at a higher valuation down the line, delivering you a tidy profit.

But just because customers are buying, doesn't mean investors will. This will, of course, minimize your ROI and the decarbonization you are trying to drive forward with your capital.

That happened when I examined an agriculture company who worked with farmers on carbon, commodity sales, and farm management improvements. The company had a lofty valuation, after raising nearly $1 billion in capital, and had grown revenues from about $150 million in 2020 to nearly $1 billion in 2022. At first blush, they seemed to me and the broader market like a great investment opportunity poised for an IPO.

But when I talked with their customers and employees, I grew concerned. Several customers told me they had not seen the value they expected, and they were not planning to renew. Existing and former employers also told me that the number of farmers they had enrolled as customers was far less than the number that engaged in the climate programs.

The proposition seemed to me to be all sizzle, and no steak. I politely thanked my contact for the opportunity and passed. With a high valuation and an underperforming product, I anticipated an inevitable crash. It came in 2023, when the company reported its valuation had fallen by nearly 95 percent!

These dual areas of demand can be mastered. You need to understand the customers, when to think about regulations, when to ignore them, and what differentiates the investment you're considering from the competition. When you understand these aspects of demand, you gain greater understanding of the investment's potential to increase in value.

You will also gain a better understanding of the potential scale of the decarbonization impact. In Principle 1, I discussed how to build and forecast your CRP. That forecast is based on how many people will use the solution being offered, allowing you to gauge whether the company's prediction is accurate and how realistic are the decarbonization estimates.

Make the Calls

I am not being entirely metaphoric when I advise you to hop on the phone and call customers. You can use Zoom, Microsoft Teams, Google Meets or whatever communication technology you choose. I find as many customers as I can, eschewing the ones the company pointed me to.

I did precisely this with Groundwork BioAg (Groundwork) a prospective investment, and I couldn't be happier with the results. Groundwork sells Rootella™, a series of products made from mycorrhiza fungus. Farmers coat seeds in Rootella™, and it drives higher crop yields that are more robust and climate resilient, and reduces fertilizer, water, input demand and cost. Additionally, through a symbiotic process between the crop and the fungus, a tremendous amount of carbon is permanently sequestered in soil, as well.

I liked the overall proposition when Groundwork came to me, but I had seen a lot of biologicals over the past ten years as had members of my team at ClimateIC—and none have managed to grow successfully enough to reach Gigacorn status or even prospectively so.

I called several of Groundwork's customers in Brazil, the US, Ukraine, among others. The reports were universally positive. I repeatedly heard reports about bigger crop yields, reduced fertilizer use and water needs and healthier soil.

One customer really blew my mind. He was an agricultural engineer who had recently taken over his parents' farm in Brazil. He told me that they started using Rootella™ on 100 hectares (220 acres) of their 10,000-hectare farm to test it out.

"In that year," he told me, "We had a 100 percent increase in our casava crop yield. It's unheard of. It doubled! Doubled my yield while using 10 percent less fertilizer."

The next year, he expanded to 1,000 hectares and again, doubled his crop yield. This time, he reduced his fertilizer by half. In the third year, he was using Rootella™ across his entire farm, and he had reduced his fertilizer use by 80 percent—all this during the worst drought in Brazil's history.

With calls like that, how could we not consider an investment?

The best part came when I called the CEO to tell him I wanted to invest. I shared with him the stories I had heard, and he was amazed. He knew his product was good, but he only had conversations with distributors, not the farmers themselves. It opened his eyes to the real people using the product, and the incredible results they were seeing.

Groundwork demonstrates the importance of conversations with customers. But what happens if those customers only exist because demand is generated through regulation?

Demand Should Stand Independent of Regulation

Regulation may seem like a great mover of customers. After all, regulation can be very powerful and can create new markets, in some cases, they anoint marketplace winners. But if customers are only using a product because of regulation, the demand can be cut off at the knees as regulators tear down or enact new legislation.

That's why it is important to ensure that the product or service of your potential investment has sufficient demand whether or not there are regulations in place to stimulate demand.

Let's say an investment comes to you looking for equity, a cash infusion. They tell you, "We've got incredible demand, because the government's regulating it." Well, governments come and go, and policies constantly change. If a regulation vanishes after the next election, or that policy shifts to focus on a new sector, where does that leave your investment?

If the answer is, "in the dust," you have a political and regulatory risk that needs to be understood and managed.

Some demand is driven by regulation, and some demand is driven by need. The balance and interplay between the two must be assessed to understand the likely demand.

- If there *is no regulation* and there is need, there will be some critical mass of buyers.
- If there *is regulation* and there is need, there will likely be a steady supply of buyers.

Between these two scenarios exists a sort of Death Valley. It happens when regulation is proposed. While there is a customer need, as regulation is slowly introduced, buyers stop in their tracks. They want clarity on what the rules are going to look like before they invest in a new product or service. If you get caught in that valley, it can be the end of your investment.

When evaluating a potential investment, you have to be mindful of the landscape into which you're investing. Ask yourself whether there's sufficient demand for the given solution in a changing regulatory market. Is the demand driven by need? Is it solving a real problem for its customers? Or is it only providing a temporary fix to the current landscape? Then, ask yourself how the regulatory market is changing and whether you might get caught in the crossfire.

I have found myself caught in Death Valley, knowing the company I've invested in will only be successful if the government removed a roadblock through legislation. Waiting to find out whether or not regulations will pass is agonizing. Save yourself a lot of headaches and don't invest in companies that may land in the Valley.

I remember when governments around the world were leaning in on methane control. Over 150 governments signed the Methane Pledge to cut emissions by 30 percent by 2030.[65] Why? Methane is a very potent greenhouse gas, punching well above its weight at over 28 times the global warming potential of carbon dioxide over a 100-year time frame (refer back to the section in Chapter 2, Greenhouse Gas Emissions, for a reminder). Methane is also a short-lived greenhouse gas, with its impact lasting less than thirty years in the atmosphere. So, eliminating methane emissions from the economy would result in nearly a 0.5-degree Celsius reduction in global heating.[66] This is very significant.

The impact of eliminating methane paired with the adoption by over 150 governments to the Methane Pledge compelled my colleagues to research opportunities to invest in climatech that can eliminate methane emissions from agriculture, industrial processes, waste management and, of course, the oil & gas industry. Drones, cameras, chemical sensors, flaring systems. You name it and my colleagues looked at it, eventually making an investment in a very impressive methane detection system. With hundreds of their devices deployed in the field and federal legislation in review by the US Environmental Protection Agency, the thesis was clear. The investment was made.

But a very important lesson was learned. Pending legislation can be a one-way trip to Death Valley. Especially if the company does not have enough cash to wait for the legislation to be confirmed and then enacted and enforced. In this case, buyers sat on the sidelines waiting for the legislation to pass. With the US Supreme Court then striking down the Chevron Doctrine, essentially hamstringing the US EPA from regulating methane, the company floundered.[67] Existing customers were maintained, but no growth would be seen.

To keep up with macro-level trends in climate legislation, educate yourself about national and supra-national programs such as the Inflation Reduction Act (a $370 billion commitment), the EU Green Deal (a $700 billion commitment), and the Canada Growth Fund (a $15 billion commitment), as well as more discreet regulation that is often sector-specific such as state and national legislation related to the internal combustion engine or tax breaks for carbon capture projects.[68,69,70] Each piece of legislation offers insight into the financial, operational, and legal types of risk and opportunity that extend. They can either help you identify Death Valley or the promised land. This line between the two can be thin, so use caution and consult the market, customers, legislators and experts before making your investment decision.

LEGISLATION AS TAILWIND

When we invested in LineVision, no regulation was in place to encourage buyers. Instead, buyers were incentivized by how much the product improved electrical grid performance. Buyers lined up to outfit their grids with LineVision's solution because it worked.

It was amazing when the Inflation Reduction Act was announced. It included a multibillion-dollar e-grid initiative that supercharged LineVision's growth. This was nice to have, and one that we did not predict in the near-term. Legislation helped nudge the dial, but it wasn't the main reason to invest and never should be.

When researching regulations, ensure you don't put the cart before the horse. Sometimes, people move on proposed regulations that have not yet passed, but many regulations die on their way to the floor. If it doesn't pass, those promised customers don't materialize, meaning there's neither a demand nor a future for your investment.

Differentiate From Your Competition

Finally, calculate an investment's differentiation from the competition to ensure demand. What makes your potential investment unique, valuable and enduring? Why does it stand out from the crowd?

This is an incredibly challenging area, because so many companies are championing new technology. The thing about a pioneer is that the copycats and clones show up fast. If they're cheaper or more efficient, you may find yourself floating upside down in the water.

A good example is with Measurement, Reporting and Verification (MRV) technologies. It is important and very necessary to measure, report, and verify carbon emission reductions accurately. The necessity comes from the need to account for emissions to meet regulatory requirements in some jurisdictions, and the carbon credit verification and validation process.

The need for MRV led to a surge in companies trying to develop cost effective solutions. Every company was sure it could do it better, and soon they found themselves competing for investment, customers, and talent – with the conventional market, other segments of the climatech market, but most significantly, with one another.

While the first solution, let's call them MRV Inc., was making, say, 80 percent margins, the next few companies to jump in with new solutions decided they had to sell at half price to break into the market. They were only making 40 percent margins, but they were happy with that. As Jeff Bezos so famously said, "Your margin is my opportunity." So, companies willing to cut their margins devoured the customer base of MRV Inc. MRV Inc. must respond. They think, "Well, I have a lot of cash on hand, I can survive." So, they drop their prices and settle for a 30 percent margin.

That started a race to the bottom. Soon, the MRV industry found they required more and more equity to subsidize the cost of servicing customers and to maintain or grow market share.

Industry after industry will show you that commoditization spells death knell for competition in any sector. The only way to win in that space is for someone to gather enough cash to buy up a critical mass of their competitors and raise the prices again. One powerful example of a company that mastered this consolidation strategy is Waste Management, Inc. in the environmental services industry. Over the years, Waste Management systematically acquired a significant number of smaller competitors, consolidating their position as the dominant player in waste disposal, recycling, and environmental services. By gaining a critical mass of assets and competitors, they were able to scale their operations, increase pricing power, and maintain a competitive edge. This strategic consolidation helped them dominate an industry where commoditization had threatened smaller players with lower margins. They turned a fragmented industry into a cash-generating powerhouse.

It is only a matter of time before a company like Persefoni or Greenly could do the same in the MRV market. They may acquire smaller competitors to consolidate market leadership, especially as the growing demand for precise carbon measurement data has led to the emergence of a vast array of companies driving the commoditization of MRV. Companies with strong financial backing and innovative tech solutions could be well-positioned to consolidate and dominate. It would streamline offerings, set the industry standard, accelerate company growth, expand their influence and allow them to raise prices.

Get Smart About Your Competition

Before you invest, you must understand your investment's total competitive landscape. What else is out there? Can the company clearly communicate uniqueness and competitive advantages?

I've seen many investments that are interesting opportunities, but they have thirty or forty competitors in the marketplace or could be disrupted by long-standing and cash rich incumbents. When the playing field is that crowded, it's hard to argue that any one solution will rise to the top.

THE COMPETITIVE MOAT

How well a company is protected from rivals is called the company's competitive moat The moat may be wider or narrower depending on factors such as IP, trade secrets, relationships with customers, time in the market, first-mover advantage, and speed of innovation, among others.

Companies must be really clear about how they're unique, and how they plan to maintain their competitive advantage over time. As rivals enter the field, pioneering their own version of the solution or product, how will your company stay in the lead? How will they keep their customers, and continue to attract new ones? Can they continue to innovate and bring on the next evolution of their product?

One great way to ensure a competitive advantage is through intellectual property (IP). IP often refers to patents, but also includes trade secrets and the strategy employed to protect the company's IP. What exactly does the company own—and how easy will it be for others to copy or circumvent it? You should ask questions like:

- Where is the company's IP protected geographically? Is it just in one country, or is it in many countries? Are the countries in which the IP is protected the major markets?
- How easily can people go around, copy, or modify the company's product or service?
- If the company has IP protection, like a patent, when will it expire?
- Is making the product or providing the service capital intensive, and thus dissuasive for competitors?

There's a company in Canada that refers to themselves "the Expedia of Logistics." They built a platform so logistics operators (service companies that transport goods) all around the world could find the best way to get their products from point A to B. That platform included a carbon profile alongside the price of shipping that helped operators choose the least carbon intensive route to move goods. They thought they were offering a unique service that would have huge customer demand and marketed its IP as a part of the attractiveness of the offering for investors.

When my team did some research, we discovered that a significant number of incumbent logistics companies already offered a carbon profile on their existing tools—they just weren't advertising it. These tools had huge built in audiences...and had existed for years before this startup. Regrettably, this opportunity didn't have the unique proposition or IP protection it thought it had—and that made investing in this company too risky.

It was a shame because the company CEO was a celebrated and internationally recognized thought leader in the space having advised the United Nations on the potential to decarbonize the logistics industry. He had put in the time and much of his own money to develop this tool, but others simply were in the market earlier than his company with the key relationships needed to win.

If you can't get insight into the customer, don't understand the regulatory risk and competitive landscape, well then you can't assess demand. And that makes the company a bad, or at least a high risk, investment for you. Not because the company is doomed to fail, but because you should never underwrite investments you don't understand.

On the other hand, if you understand the customer, have clarity of legislation, both pending and active, successfully map the competition and find the IP strategy to be bullet proof, you may have a great investment on your hands.

In the next chapter, I'll tell you how to create even more value for a company you've invested in.

Support investments with strategic guidance for *long-term profitability* and decarbonization.

CHAPTER 7

PRINCIPLE 4

CREATE VALUE WITH CARBON

"We are not just investing in the future; we are creating it."

— Ray Anderson, Interface Founder and former White House advisor

A Dining Ecosystem

When you invest in a company, do you take it as it is and leave it alone, or do you share your skills, knowledge, network, and strategic insights to help turn it into what you know it can and should be, remarkable?

Thomas Keller, the chef and owner of the acclaimed French Laundry restaurant in California Wine Country, is an expert in the kitchen who understands the chemistry of cooking, flavor palettes, and industry trends. He knows how to delight diners with new experiences. But when he acquired The French Laundry in 1994, he didn't just start cooking: He brought with him a philosophy of farm-to-table.[71]

Toward his goal, Keller built a network of local farmers, artisans, and suppliers to source sustainable, seasonal, and organic foods and ingredients. He established a community with its own system, and taught his staff how to best use that system, and he taught customers the benefit of farm-to-table for memorable dining experiences rarely experienced elsewhere.

Keller is more than just an owner/chef: He adds value beyond his culinary and management expertise. In addition to focusing on unique and memorable dishes, he personalized the dining experience with attention to detail and iconic dishes of nearly unmatched quality. This catapulted The French Laundry to the very top of the lists of the world's most iconic restaurants.

Create Value in Your Investments

As a Gigacorn Hunter, you should be like Keller and make an asset, your investment, more valuable than you found it by leveraging what and who you know. If you sit on the board of the company in which you invest, you are singularly positioned to uncover and recommend opportunities to add value.

This is the fourth principle of Gigacorn hunting: create value. Support investments with strategic guidance for long-term profitability and decarbonization.

The three aspects to creating value are:

1. Define the pathways to creating value;
2. Quantify the value and apply it to your models; and
3. Increase the amount and rate of the CRP.

Creating value starts by offering strategic support. It is the help you provide beyond the provision of capital; beyond the cash you invest. It is the overall enterprise value that you can enhance by leveraging decarbonization. As a Gigacorn Hunter, you are uniquely qualified to do this.

In most cases, you will be considering investing in a technology of which the potential is not yet fully realized. You can't just assess its profit potential based on what the company knows to be true about itself today, as I pointed out in Principle 2, Make a Profit. You also need to analyze ways the company may not yet have identified to make profits or optimize opportunities. As a climate capitalist, it's up to you to introduce specific concepts that can either remove, or in some cases, remove all doubt about the company's potential, specifically, it's CRP.

When you can do that, you provide the company with the advantage of deeper intelligence and deeper insight regarding how much additional value can be created, and what mechanisms will enable them through its CRP. You will empower the company with what it needs to know to maximize the CRP and make wise choices to enhance company value.

Finding Value in Decarbonization

A traditional investor looks over the financials and says, "I can see they're going to sell 1000 units at $5000 each this year. That's fantastic, and it will mean $5 million in revenue."

A climate capitalist would agree, and add to this by saying, "I see that the decarbonization they're going to deliver through each of these units is 5000 tons. That's five million tons of carbon. Can it be monetized? Can it be used to market the company or by its customers to enhance their performance? What price will the market pay for this type of carbon today and for the foreseeable future? Can we increase the decarbonization so these opportunities go further?"

Creating value leads to a higher company valuation once the investment executes on its business plan—and, of course, this yields a greater return for you as an investor.

The ability to identify how to create value also leads to the potential to invest at a more competitive valuation than other investors, putting you in the position to win the investment opportunity. Yes, investors often compete for deals.

When trying to lead and secure an investment, investors submit to the potential investment what is referred to as a Term Sheet, a legal document that lays out the various conditions of the offer. The conditions, or terms, typically include things such as the total investment commitment size (how much you are willing to invest), the value assigned to the company (what you think the company is worth at the time of your investment), the number of board seats required, and a host of other bells and whistles. Many deals hinge on the bells and whistles, but more commonly, the valuation is a deciding factor.

The reason is that the valuation will determine how much the existing shareholders will be able to mark up their initial investment on their books. In the simplest terms, if I invested when the company was valued at $10 million and now it is valued at $100 million, that is an excellent mark-up of 10X, in investor parlance. With that performance, I would be celebrated by my fellow investors. That is why, typically, the higher the valuation, the more compelling the offer as existing investors clamor for the mark-up opportunity. Not always, but often.

So, when you know how you can help create value and you understand the growth potential of the opportunity better than competing investors, you can submit a Term Sheet with a higher valuation to better ensure your likelihood of winning the deal. While others might see the valuation as too high, you understand why it is well-priced.

Remember that the contrary can be true, too.

If you don't understand how to create value or misunderstand the value creation opportunities for your investment, the investment may well fail to achieve its full potential or even take a wrong turn and company value may erode. Future investors may then buy-in at a discounted valuation to your last round and you can go from a 10X to a 0.1X because your investment underperformed. If we look back to the last example, if you invest at a $10 million valuation and the next investor comes in and picks the company up on the cheap with a $1 million valuation...well, forget about the ribbons and champagne in that scenario.

Understanding how to create value helps ensure that you can bid competitively, maximize value, and make informed decisions about companies likely to increase in value. You must educate yourself, understand the pathways through which value can be created with carbon, and then quantify the value of it in your financial models.

Define the Pathways to Value Creation

In Principle 1, we discussed how to measure carbon but only briefly touched on value creation through carbon. Now, you need to apply this knowledge and evaluate the pathways through which the investment will drive decarbonization. This will allow you, as a Gigacorn Hunter, to determine how the decarbonization can be monetized. This may take many forms, influenced by the Three Rs of Decarbonization (Reduce, Replace, and Remove).

When you can evaluate all the pathways through which the investment has the potential to drive decarbonization, it allows you to understand how carbon can be monetized over the life of your investment. These pathways may include:

- Sell carbon offsets.
- Sell carbon insets.
- Sell regulated carbon credits.
- Tie credits into products and services, rendering them low, neutral, or carbon negative.
- Donate carbon credits to others.
- Operate as a low, neutral, or carbon-negative company.
- Leverage marketing potential.

Remember that all pathways are not created equal. It is very important to understand that not all carbon is equal, either. Each has a different level of quality. In addition to determining which ones add value, you should measure the quality of both the pathway and the carbon.

My friend Alex Pernin, CEO of carbon finance company Green Star Royalties, explains it this way. "Carbon is not like gold. 99.9 percent pure gold is completely uniform and consistent both physically and in monetary value no matter where in the world it is found. Carbon is much more like diamonds. Each diamond is uniquely priced as per the physical characteristics of its cut, clarity, color and carat."

Perhaps this is another coincidence, but how tidy it is that diamonds are made of pure carbon. This makes the comparison all that more apt.

For carbon, the equivalent to cut, clarity, color and carat for diamonds are:

1. **Additional**. Would the carbon avoidance or reduction have occurred without the financial value delivered through the sale of carbon?
2. **Permanent**. Is the carbon sequestered permanently (more than 100-1000 years)?
3. **Measurable**. Is the carbon removal or avoidance quantifiable?
4. **Verifiable**. Can an independent source certify the carbon has been removed or avoided?
5. **Scalable**. Can the carbon be avoided or removed at a cost and speed required to avoid the ravages of climate change?

When the pathway is to sell carbon offsets, insets or, for instance, understanding the quality of carbon will help you more accurately evaluate the claims of any given company, and the total potential value that can be created. For a more comprehensive set of criteria to consider, you can also refer to the Core Carbon Principles of The Integrity Council for the Voluntary Carbon Market.[72]

IS YOUR PATHWAY FUTURE-PROOF?

Pay attention to carbon market shifts. Who's buying what and where is the money going? In the early 2020s, we saw an interesting trend as some companies shifted away from carbon offsets to carbon insets.

It has continued to amaze me how interchangeably the terms offsets, insets and credits are used, but they are each very different things.

Carbon offsets refer to reductions or removals made by one company that are then sold to another. A business can purchase a carbon offset in tons from one company the successfully removed carbon instead of reducing its own emissions. It is a tactic often used by businesses in an effort to achieve net-zero carbon emissions, an accounting exercise that establishes a balance between the carbon emitted and the carbon avoided or removed by the company. Carbon insets mean that a company has undertaken an activity, which resulted in carbon being avoided or removed within its own operations or supply chain. Instead of selling the reductions, it takes advantage of them internally toward their decarbonization efforts. This may include the company achieving net-zero operations or allowing the company to sell no- or low-carbon products or services.

In the early 2020s, Unilever and several other large consumer packaged goods (CPG) companies abandoned carbon offsets altogether to focus on reductions within their own supply chains.[73] As of this writing, the jury was still out as to whether or not this was an effective strategy for Unilever and the rest of the CPGs that went along.

My point is that you need to gauge the health and complexities of the overall carbon market to know how to value insets, offsets, and other carbon instruments, among many other factors.

The Risk of Climate Credits

You should conduct your due diligence to ensure your carbon reduction pathways comply with the five carbon quality requirements listed above. If you don't you risk losing everything.

This happened in March 2023 when South Pole, one of the world's leading carbon project developers and carbon offset marketers, was accused by *Bloomberg Businessweek* of exaggerating its climate claims related to forest protection projects, raising credibility concerns with the voluntary carbon market.[74]

Swiss-based South Pole operates in carbon credits, particularly through its Afforestation, Reforestation, and Revegetation (ARR) projects. The company collaborates with landowners to prevent deforestation and to replant trees in areas previously deforested by human activity, earning carbon credits as trees capture carbon through photosynthesis.

The problem emerged with a project in Zimbabwe where critics, as reported by *Bloomberg*, accused South Pole of overstating its carbon credits. Allegations included claims that fewer trees were being planted than reported, and that the company claimed to protect land from logging where logging was neither occurring nor planned. While South Pole defended its claims as legitimate, the controversy raised concerns about the transparency and accuracy of its reporting. The broader carbon offset market, particularly projects like ARR, faced scrutiny as investors and the public questioned the validity of how carbon credits were being measured, verified, and marketed.

In addition to criticism of South Pole, the *Bloomberg* article highlighted that investors also shared responsibility for not ensuring that the credits were properly vetted for permanence, measurability, and verifiability. The controversy underscored the importance of rigorous due diligence by all stakeholders involved in carbon markets.

Overall, the controversy tarnished South Pole's reputation, leading to broader questions about the integrity of the voluntary carbon market. If you do the same thing as what South Pole was accused of doing, you risk the credibility of your company's carbon assets and overall valuation tanking, and a huge loss of profit.

Keep in mind that some pathways may be permanent, verifiable, and measurable but are too small to be worth exploring on your own. What I mean is that the cost of developing and operating a carbon credit program can exceed the revenues you might receive, so it is not an economically rational pursuit. Of course, a Gigacorn Hunter's investments should generate an extraordinary amount of carbon in which case this caveat does not apply. But there are cases when the amount of carbon generated to become economically viable happens later in the investment period. In such cases, it may be that management of the carbon strategy includes a variety of the pathways at different points in time. For instance, start with marketing the low-carbon benefits of the product and then transition to carbon offsetting or insetting.

Once you have explored all pathways to creating value for a company, you are ready to calculate the specific pathways available to your potential investment.

Quantify Value and Apply It to Your Models

As we discussed in Principle 2, Make a Profit, it's important to know how an investment will generate returns. Conventional financial models are the beginning of that calculus. However, as a Gigacorn Hunter, your job is to incorporate into your financial models what is neglected by conventional investors, such as carbon (and other environmental and social attributes we will explore in Chapter 8).

These often-neglected items are commodities that have monetizable value in the benefits they provide. For example, climatech might enhance water quality or reduce air pollution. When you bring those elements into your financial model, you gain a wider view of the technology's impact. Quantifying the value created for the investment—and the customers of the investment—makes you a better, more insightful, and prosperous investor. One who knows how to value the investment and create value for the investment more readily than those who do not identify pathways and the monetization of each.

DON'T RELY JUST ON CARBON

Remember that your carbon calculus should only exist as an addendum to the financial models you have completed by following Principle 2. Never rely on additional revenue through carbon to drive your investment decision. As we noted in Chapter 6, or Principle 3 Ensure Demand, the company must stand on its own with or without regulation. The same holds true for the ability to monetize carbon.

Some climate investors seek to support one-trick carbon ponies that only generate carbon credits. That does not seem to me to be a wise investment. When you start to build out your financial models, you will quickly see that a company like this only appears to be a good investment once you add the carbon reduction potential into the equation. Indeed, it can only be a good investment by including the carbon revenue as the technology does nothing else. It generates no other revenue.

It is not an investment segment in which I dedicate my time because a company with no strong underlying business, product, or service is often less resilient to market changes and less prepared with options to allow the company to pivot when surprising events pop up. Take the change in the voluntary carbon market value from 2022 to 2023. It lost over 60 percent of its value over that period.[75] Imagine if your revenues were solely dependent on carbon and losing 60 percent of your revenue within twelve months. Generating carbon credits can be part of your strategy, but not the whole of it. It is like macaroni without the cheese. Sure, it is edible, but would you really want to eat it?

Take, for example, two companies: Climeworks and Air Company. Each captures carbon, but they do it very differently and produce two different outcomes.

Climeworks operates in a segment of the carbon space known as carbon removal. This is characterized as directly and permanently removing carbon from the atmosphere. Whereas Air Carbon is a carbon capture & utilization (CCU) company, a process that captures emissions directly from industrial emission sources before they enter the atmosphere.

Climeworks uses fans to draw in carbon dioxide from the air, compress it, and inject it deep underground using a process called carbon capture & storage (CCS). The problem is that the process is currently estimated to cost more than $1000 per ton of sequestered carbon. Are they removing atmospheric carbon? Absolutely. Is that necessary to ameliorate the climate crisis? Absolutely! Looking at our five carbon criteria, could the process happen without selling carbon offsets? No. Is it permanent? The science indicates it is. Measurable? Yes, without a doubt. Is it verifiable? You bet! You can see it flowing into the storage caverns.

But at more than $1000 per ton, how scalable is this business? What are the odds that a much less expensive solution will come along and offer the same or better quality of carbon removal at a fraction of the price? I would estimate that at about 100 percent.

In fact, such technologies are already here in the form of nature-based and highly technical industrial solutions. Currently, there are several well-capitalized companies buying carbon credits from Climeworks and gaining deeper experience and exposure to these and other quality carbon removals. It is possible that Climeworks will find itself unable to sell its carbon removals and cease to grow as these buyers shift investing from limited quantities of $1000 per ton carbon to abundant carbon removal credits priced at more reasonable $20-100 per ton.

Of course, continued investment in companies like Climeworks will undoubtedly moderate the cost profile of their carbon removals and the underlying technology: But starting at over $1000 a ton of carbon, there is a long way to go, perhaps longer than your investment horizon and also, quite possibly, longer than buyers are willing to wait and longer than the climate can wait, too.

Now consider Air Company, a marketplace darling and one-time Time magazine cover model. It captures carbon emissions directly from industrial sources like flue gases preventing it's release into the atmosphere. This is CCU. Air Company uses the carbon it captures to manufacture products like Air Vodka, Air Eau de Parfum (perfume), and jet fuel. Have fossil fuels been extracted from the Earth and processed to create these products? No, and that's a good thing. It has reduced the demand for virgin fossil fuels. Nicely done. That easily supports the notion of more carbon-efficient production, a reduction technology. So, they are reducing emissions and selling a product. Two elements we said moments ago are important.

The challenge is that the priority before us is to reduce the atmospheric concentration of carbon to avoid and reverse the impacts of climate change. In this case, Air Company recycles atmospheric carbon, but it doesn't replace or remove it. We have at this writing, more than 420 parts per million (ppm) of carbon dioxide in our atmosphere. We need to lower that number to under 350 ppm, not just pause its advance. You will notice that recycle is not one of the 3 R's of decarbonization for this very reason. Recycling can be part of the solution, to be sure, but it can really only be a part of it if the technology reduces emissions. If it does not, the role of climatech that recycles carbon may only be significant once it crosses a critical threshold of displacement of conventional products, or once the atmospheric concentration of carbon dioxide is low enough and declining at a rate sufficient to avoid the impacts of climate change. A mass balance of all carbon emission sources and sinks would help us all to determine precisely the size and timing of the role recycling can play.

I should point out that the climate challenge is enormous, and it is an all-hands-on-deck point in time if we are to solve the challenge. Investing in technologies like Climeworks and Air Company is critical to reduce risk and deploy solutions, but it is not where I spend my time. Governments and other public and private market investors continue to invest here, and it is welcome and something to recognize and celebrate.

Increase the Amount and Rate of Carbon Reduction Potential

Your in-depth understanding of potential CRP pathways makes you a valuable investment partner. Your knowledge enables you to influence business strategy, as your insights may help the company allocate capital more efficiently and create more value for the investment.

A true Gigacorn Hunter is not just an investor, but also a value-added partner.

Your biggest challenge is to prove your worth to the companies you want to invest in and to advise. When you have that experience and that proven history, it may become a top reason that a company chooses you as its lead investor. You have something to offer that other investors don't have. But it's okay if you don't have the experience yet, because you can prove your expertise by showing what you have uncovered during due diligence. You demonstrate your pathway mapping and show strategic opportunities to enhance their business. Note that this should be done with humility and honesty. There will always be more for you to learn. I know that is the case for me.

My fund portfolio, ClimateIC, includes a company called Mysa. It makes a smart thermostat for decentralized HVAC systems (think window-mounted air conditioners, baseboard heaters, in-floor heating, and heat pumps). It enables users to better monitor and control their energy use, reducing electricity use by about 15 percent.

When Mysa was first introduced to us, I found the opportunity to reduce energy use by 15 percent interesting but not wildly compelling. It seemed unlikely to become a Gigacorn or reach the mCRP. However, during the diligence process, Joshua Green, the CEO, mentioned that their technology included an ability for local utilities to enroll homes into demand response programs without using additional instruments, software, or technology. My ears perked up, and I dug in deeper to explore

Local utilities see surges in use during peak hours, most significantly early in the morning when everyone is getting ready for work and school, and when everyone comes home from their day and flips on lights, computers, laundry machines and so on.

Utilities can predict these surges and are prepared to meet them by firing up peaking plants, power plants that can be turned on and off with little challenge. Many are powered by fossil fuels like coal and natural gas. If utilities can throttle energy in people's homes by a small amount, individuals won't even notice the difference. But the utility? They can reduce the need for peaking plans or even take the entire peaking plant offline.

When we walked the Mysa team through the value of the demand response program to their CRP and the sales proposition to local utilities, it changed Mysa's strategy. In the months and years that followed, they dedicated additional capital to developing their demand response program. Additionally, they leaned in closer to our ClimateIC team, seeking our operational management advice.

As you look for ways to advise a company on its CRP, try finding opportunities that are perpetual and not just a one-hit wonder. If we had only been able to help Mysa take a single power plant offline, it wouldn't have been such a huge win. But every utility that uses Mysa will have the potential to take peaking plants offline and continue to deliver CRP year-over-year.

From a long-term value creation perspective, your solutions should deliver returns through carbon perpetually. That is how you effectively impact the long-term financial and existential sustainability of the investment.

You also want to explore other ways your asset can create value. What are the co-benefits of a potential investment?

We'll talk about that in the next chapter.

Find Co-benefits beyond **carbon, including environmental** and **social factors,** to maximize the **potential return** and **impact** of any investment.

CHAPTER 8

PRINCIPLE 5
FIND CO-BENEFITS

"The whole is greater than the sum of its parts"

— Aristotle, ancient Greek philosopher

A Thriving New City

In the late 1970s, my grandfather, Peter Budd, founded a landmark video game arcade in Toronto called Funland Arcade, which he owned and operated for over 40 years. But like other North American cities, pinball, the original arcade game, was illegal or highly regulated.

Since the late '30s, many governments saw pinball as an opportunity for mobsters to corrupt youth and promote gambling, but my grandfather still pressed ahead. Though police raided Funland from time-to-time, my grandfather lobbied with determination to reverse the laws.

One of his key arguments was that an arcade could help transform Toronto's Yonge & Dundas Streets downtown corridor into a vibrant entertainment district. He also believed an arcade parlor could deliver a fortune one-quarter at a time, an argument that convinced no one but an accountant. To convince the government to change, he touted co-benefits, coining the slogan, "Yonge Street is Fun Street," and painting a picture of a vibrant corridor featuring theaters, record stores, and other recreational destinations.

He helped persuade authorities to reverse prior decisions against arcade games. Before long, he realized his dream, and along with other iconic locals like Sam the Record Man and The Eaton Center, the area transformed into what is now known as Dundas Square. Replete with new businesses and affluent customers, the area has become a mecca for shopping, restaurants, education, and entertainment businesses.

My grandfather accomplished all this because he was aware of the co-benefits of his arcade parlor. He understood how to leverage the neighborhood to increase the value of his own asset while contributing to a greater good.

Exploring Co-Benefits for the World's Good

Like my grandfather's arcade and his vision for community improvement, climate is inextricably linked to every aspect of our civilization. Energy issues are climate issues. Food issues are climate issues. Water issues are climate issues. Pollution issues are climate issues. And yes, poverty issues are climate issues. This is because climate change is a risk multiplier. It exacerbates the severity and increases the likelihood of issues.

But it also means that solving climate change can relieve the pressure on these environmental and social issues. A Gigacorn Hunter's work extends beyond decarbonization and into other critical environmental, social, and economic factors.

This leads to my Fifth Principle for a Climate Investor, Find Co-benefits: Reveal the benefits beyond carbon, including environmental and social factors, to maximize the potential return and impact of any investment.

As a Gigacorn Hunter, your focus is climate and always should be when it comes to your investments. You are a climate investor, of course. But your eyes must also remain open to other possibilities.

Your investment can and should drive benefits beyond carbon reduction. You will need to recognize these co-benefits and how they can create value for your investments.

To follow this fifth principle, you want to:

1. Inventory the Co-Benefits;
2. Gauge the ROI of Co-Benefits; and
3. Focus on Decarbonization.

When you can do that, you will be well positioned to identify additional value creation opportunities and the implications of variables such as social equity, food security and water abundance. This will help your investment to consider strategy development and execution when making their decisions. It may also help you identify how it may become distracted by a co-benefit—and fall short of the CRP. By doing so, you become an opportunity multiplier for every company in which you invest.

If you remain blind to the co-benefit possibilities, you will never understand the true potential of the businesses in which you want to invest. You will also remain blind to the risks. A business may deliver phenomenal impacts for one environmental factor while compromising another in spectacular fashion. This investment may be at risk of losing money or traction from fines, lawsuits, or negative publicity. Maybe I should call this principle Co-Benefits & Risks.

To understand the potential co-benefits at work, you must understand the interconnected social and environmental factors that each technology you evaluate for investment influences. A great place to start is by using the United Nations Sustainable Development Goals (UN SDGs) as a framework to conduct inventory.[76]

Inventory the Co-Benefits

In 2015, most of the world's leaders adopted the 2030 Agenda for Sustainable Development, which included seventeen goals under a framework known as the SDGs. The goals are unique in that they call for action by all countries to promote prosperity while protecting the planet.

My friend and colleague Chris Coulter, CEO of Globescan and a leading authority on global sustainability, has a deep understanding of the intersection between business, government, and civil society. Under his leadership, Globescan has helped shape critical conversations about the future we want for both society and the planet. Chris shared this insightful perspective with me about the UN SDGs:

"Leading up to their launch in 2015, the world had a serious discussion about the future we collectively want. It involved government, civil society and business and resulted in remarkable consensus about the future of society and the planet. While we are well behind hitting those ambitious targets, we still have time to make up progress and I expect there will be a significant push up to 2030 to deliver on many of the 17, almost all of which are connected to transitioning to a low carbon, nature-rich economy."

His vision and experience highlight the urgency and opportunity we have to deliver on these critical global goals, but also the opportunity and the nexus between these goals.

The SDGs are a framework of environmental and social issues I use to identify the co-benefits and risks of a potential investment. (FYI – Goal thirteen is Climate Action.)

Good climate capitalists understand which environmental and social factors might influence your investment either positively or negatively. How might any of these SDGs drive enterprise value creation or destruction, and how might it improve or harm its CRP?

"The Sustainable Development Goals"

I have rejected companies with great CRPs because they pose, or may pose, a negative impact on other SDGs.

One investment opportunity I explored early on involved a company with a groundbreaking solution to address the problem of methane emissions from cattle. Methane, as you know, is a potent greenhouse gas with a Global Warming Potential 28 times that of carbon dioxide, and finding ways to reduce it is critical for mitigating climate change. The company's innovation was a feed additive for livestock that significantly reduced methane emissions from cattle digestion. Their pitch was compelling: lower greenhouse gas emissions from the agricultural sector, improved air quality, and a direct contribution to global climate goals. I was intrigued enough to consider investing. I dug in.

The company's early results looked promising, with pilot tests showing a dramatic reduction in methane emissions in controlled settings. Encouraged by these results, I began due diligence to better understand the long-term implications of their technology.

As I advanced in the diligence, a red flag began to wave. While the additive worked as intended to reduce methane, there were emerging concerns about its effects on soil health. The hypothesis follows that manure from livestock treated with the additive might contain residues that inhibit the growth of beneficial soil microbes or lack the nutrients needed to support soil biota and ecosystem functions. This raised red flags: Could this unintended consequence undermine the natural carbon sequestration ability of soil? Could it disrupt ecosystems critical for sustainable agriculture?

Without sufficient research to answer these questions, I realized the risks might supersede the benefits of methane reduction to potentially jeopardizing Goal 13—Climate Action, Goal 15—Life on Land, and even Goal 2—Zero Hunger. As much as I admired the company's innovation, I decided not to move forward with an investment.

The lesson was clear: even the most promising technologies must be evaluated for their full lifecycle impact to ensure they don't inadvertently create more problems than they solve.

As my friend Sophie Rouzeau, Global Director Sustainable Packaging, Mars Wrigley, always reminds me, "The smartest investments aren't just those that solve today's problems, but those that prevent tomorrow's. In the same way that stopping plastic pollution at the source is better than dealing with its aftermath, we must invest in solutions that align with the full life cycle of sustainability. It's not enough to fix one issue—we need to ensure we're not inadvertently creating another."

That experience reinforced a long-standing lesson I learned while riding my bicycle as a kid: Always look ahead. In the case of investing, you must examine the entire life cycle of the product or service to assess the positive and negative impacts. When it comes to this example, the initial product was great, and if it had stopped there, I may well have moved forward with an investment. But without the ability to understand the new product and the entirety of its life cycle, I was precluded from moving forward.

If the negatives are minor, you might want to run a risk/benefit assessment and determine what the net impact might be. Determine if the benefits outweigh the risks, and if so, by how much? Quantify how much risk are you willing to accept to gain the benefits. Wind farms are a great example. The noise generated can disturb people living or working nearby, but the clean power benefits often outweigh the noise for most people.

Where you fall on the spectrum of risks versus benefits is up to you. But, as an entrepreneur, you should know how to communicate your position—especially to your investors. This most certainly also applies to investors.

How Attractive Are the Co-Benefits?

Co-benefits are great—but can they be too attractive to the investment company's leadership?

The most effective and successful management teams are masters of focus. They know their priorities and how to ensure the company stays committed to and through execution. Many companies struggle with focus, especially when a shiny new object flashes before them. Identifying co-benefits can provide a path to value creation—but it can also be a dangerous distraction for the company's management. Once you've identified potential co-benefits, it's up to you to understand if the management team can maintain focus. Will they meet or exceed their CRP and growth targets, or reallocate resources to chase other opportunities, and end up a poor climate mitigator?

You can assess a company's likelihood of straying in a few ways:

- Determine the size of the co-benefit impact potential. How much money is the company poised to make by helping to solve the co-benefit(s)?

- Analyze the resource allocation demanded by the co-benefit. Will it require shifting focus away from the climate potential, or can the two work in tandem?
- Can multiple co-benefits take priority, or will one win out over the other or other(s)?
- How committed is management to the CRP? Are they passionate about climate change, or is this just a revenue or marketing opportunity for them?
- Is the CRP the first and/or the biggest SDG benefit it delivers?

Even if the company's primary goal doesn't align with yours, they can be a good fit if the co-benefits work in tandem. I saw that when my fund invested in MyLand.

MyLand is a soil health company. It couples soil science with technological innovation offering systems that plug into crop irrigation networks on farms. These systems isolate the farm's highly beneficial native microalgae and then replicate it to yield trillions of microalgae. It then injects the microalgae into the soil through the on-farm irrigation network, thus, dramatically increasing soil organic matter, porosity, water infiltration and retention capability, and more.

The process increases crop yield (GOAL 2: Zero Hunger), reduces water use (GOAL 6: Clean Water and Sanitation), and reduces the need for chemical fertilizers (GOAL 15: Life on Land) while also sequestering an astounding tonnage of carbon per acre (up to 16 tons of CO_2e per acre, according to the US Department of Agriculture (USDA) and the UN IPCC.[77]

When we first engaged with MyLand, carbon was a part of their story, but not their core focus. Its primary goal was regenerating soil health, but the decarbonization benefits were clear. And because the carbon sequestration benefits are a direct result of the core technology, it isn't at risk of being dropped as the company moves forward and expands.

That, plus the management team quality and financials, made MyLand a great investment—because it intensified and expanded its climate focus. An ideal situation for Gigacorn Hunters like us.

Focus on Decarbonization

It is no exaggeration to say I am inspired by at least one climate entrepreneur per week, and sometimes daily. Once you open a fund or investment vehicle and begin actively investing, you might be shocked by the speed and rate at which deals flow to you. They find you, quickly.

The challenge for Gigacorn Hunters is to beware of opportunities that come wrapped in the decarbonization flag as a disguise to get through the door.

Lots of companies offer some decarbonization benefits, but it isn't at the heart of their business. They might see decarbonization as a quick path to profit or fundraising, and they want in. Or they might consider climate to be an easier sell than their true proposition, which may be another SDG. Sometimes I suspect they think, "This tech is so amazing that if I can just get that first meeting, they'll see that even though we aren't really a climatech investment, we're still incredible. Who wouldn't want to invest in us?"

Weeding out impostors is a critical skill for Gigacorn Hunters. Be wary and grill them for the information you need to make the right decisions. If the investment is transparent and passionate about how they prioritize environmental and social impacts, their priorities, and how it relates to decarbonization, your decision-making should be fast and simple. But, in many cases you must learn how to dig deep.

Let's say a water tech company provides decarbonization benefits. They come to you and describe themselves as a climate company. But when you dig, it becomes clear that they focus is on water filtration, and the team will be spending their time optimizing filtration. Sure, they are more energy efficient than some competitors, and they do provide a sprinkling of decarbonization benefits, but the bottom line is this is a water business.

If we are a gaggle of carbon experts and we now know the team will be focused on the water sector, we would be doing ourselves and them a disservice. We won't be able to apply or maximize Principle 4, Create Value, because we are all about carbon, and they are about water. It is a simple, but critical misalignment of priorities.

Now, you may be wondering, "But what about MyLand? Isn't this the same example?"

No, it is not.

The difference is that MyLand's decarbonization is staggeringly high in volume and quality. It isn't just a co-benefit—it is the centerpiece of the company's proposition. MyLand is positioned to deliver millions of tons of carbon reductions.

That makes MyLand a wise choice to add to our portfolio, and we get to also assist with the realization of critical co-benefits. The bottom line, it has Gigacorn potential, and that is the focus.

Don't Let Greed Blur Your Focus

Of paramount importance is to not be fooled by carbon solution impostors who say the right words but lack the right focus. It can be easy to be seduced by impassioned and well marketed presentations by entrepreneurs who are attempting to finance mediocre carbon reductions.

As a Gigacorn Hunter, if our prospect doesn't hit your billion tons of reduction or your defined mCRP, you should pass.

Keep on track by making your fund mandate crystal clear. ClimateIC is a decarbonization fund. We only want solutions that can deliver on the Gigacorn promise of a billion tons of carbon reduced or avoided.

When someone comes to us with a deal that cannot deliver on what we are hunting for, it easy for us to say no.

I was approached by a company that had developed a very impressive innovative battery technology that had the potential to replace the popular lithium-ion (LIon) solution. The LIon battery is the current market leader in almost every application, from your computer and mobile phone to EVs and battery storage. One of the challenges, however, is the risk of fire from LIon batteries. While not as common as the media may make it seem, it does happen, and when it does, the fires can be very destructive and dangerous. Insurance companies have taken notice. As such, insurance premiums for major infrastructure that uses Lithium have been steadily rising.

Enter this new solution with a battery that is a fraction of the price and smaller than its Lithium competitors, is manufactured locally and–for the frosting on the cake—it presents zero risk of fire.

After several discussions with the company, my team found the pitch compelling, especially as it saw a very lucrative exit less than twenty-four months away. Of course, the challenge for us was decarbonization.

On its face the idea of installing battery backup lends itself well to the DoE. Batteries are needed to smooth the grid, power devices and so on. The challenge we identified was that this solution was focused on replacing an incumbent technology, Lithium, and not creating net new carbon reductions. So, while the company's functional pedigree and financial projections were compelling, we passed on it. There was simply no way this company could mitigate a billion tons of carbon or meet or mCRP. Would they get rich? Probably. But was it a fit for our fund? It was not.

Then there was a hydrogen company that approached my team. Basically, they wanted to produce hydrogen. Okay, now hydrogen, everybody talks about the fact that hydrogen is a clean fuel. And it really is, when you burn hydrogen, you're left with nothing but water vapor.

That's a wonderful thing. If that's the only product, the challenge is, how do you get the hydrogen in the first place? Hydrogen production is a very energy-intensive process. For the most part, you don't get out as much energy from the hydrogen as you must put into the process to make hydrogen.

So, it's an energy negative process. The are people in academia, private researchers, corporations, and not-for-profits trying to figure out how hydrogen can be generated with a positive energy balance. A positive energy balance refers to more energy being harnessed from the system than is put into source, generate and transport it. There is no shortage of people on the job.

The challenge was that this proposal came forward with a process called steam methane reforming, which is well-known and well-used. The problem with steam methane reforming is that it releases a tremendous amount of carbon monoxide and carbon dioxide in the process. So, when they approached me, they said, "Hey, we were going to produce hydrogen. And we need you to help us invest in this because the energy return and efficiency on the invested capital, well, it is just amazing."

It sounds great. Big money. Only after just a few questions it was revealed that the steam methane reforming process to be used would produce less than 50 percent net energy, meaning that the energy stored in the hydrogen was less than half the amount of energy that was required to produce the hydrogen.

In short, they would do more environmental damage than they would resolve.

So that failed the test. You must always check the quality of the claims. I call this conversation tabulation. Make sure the commentary is backed by data. Make sure you understand the scope of what they're talking about, because anybody can shrink the scope of their analysis into just a refined enough segment of their technology to say, "Look how impactful it is."

In this case, while the company was saying, "Look how efficient hydrogen is," we were thinking, "Yeah, that's wonderful. But your process releases more CO_2 than we would ever reduce, replace or remove once we consider how you make the hydrogen."

So that was that. It may have been a profitable opportunity, but without meeting the mCRP it was a clear pass.

Let me extend on this a little further. As was discussed in Chapter 4, Measure Carbon, we do not compromise the CRP for profit, and we don't compromise the profit for CRP. You do not need to. But also, we do not pick and choose how to characterize the decarbonization of a technology to fit it into our investment thesis because the profits look juicy. We look at the whole life cycle of the technology to understand the net carbon impact to guide our decisions objectively.

Having a defined operating goal makes it easy to stay on target—and helps you know whether an investment's co-benefits are right for you. That definition also helps you find partners with the same goals. That's a convenient segway to the next chapter, which is all about partnerships and collaboration.

Collaborate with other **investors** and **stakeholders**—who offer **complementary expertise**—to accelerate the **investment's velocity of value creation** and **impact**.

CHAPTER 9

PRINCIPLE 6

CO-OPETITION

"We have to let go of the notion that for Apple to win, Microsoft must lose."

— Steve Jobs, Apple founder

Rowing Together

When I was in college, I had a friend with whom I was rather competitive. We took physiology together, and he always seemed to beat me by 1 or 2 percent on each test or assignment. It irked me. (Clearly, it still does since I am mentioning it here). This battle of skills extended beyond the classroom, too. We constantly compared ourselves to see who came out on top. In our sophomore year, he invited me to join the rowing team. I was thrilled, and I signed up in the spirit of competition: I was going to show him that I could row faster and stronger than he could.

The team I was invited to join was the Eight, a boat consisting of eight oars and one person per oar. As I started to train, determined to prove just how fast and strong I was, I quickly learned something: rowing fastest accomplished nothing at all: In fact, it was counterproductive.

If we wanted to win, then we all had to row together.

If I went faster than my teammates, it threw off the entire rhythm. We weren't competing with each other—we were competing with the other boats. We still wanted to be strongest and row fastest. But we had to drive each other to row harder, faster, and stronger together. We had to cooperate without losing our competitive spirit.

The Spirit of Co-opetition

How do you balance competition and cooperation in the investing world?

The traditional investing world is one of kill or be killed. People hoard opportunities, deal flow will make or break you, and everyone is out for themselves.

In climatech, we are all aligned on decarbonization outcomes. We share a moral philosophy, and we have a vested interest in lifting others up and into this sphere. But we're also still competing for capital. We're competing for deals. To excel and move forward at the pace and scope we need to in climatech to solve the wicked problem of climate change, we must balance these two fundamentally opposed concepts of competition and cooperation.

As Gigacorn Hunters, we work with others to accelerate the pace of value creation and impact.

That can be difficult, but it's possible when we embrace the spirit of co-opetition. What exactly is co-opetition? It's a combination of cooperation and competition, a strategy where organizations collaborate in certain areas while competing in others.

The sixth principle of the climate capitalist is Co-opetition: Collaborate with other investors and stakeholders—who offer complementary expertise—to accelerate the investment's velocity of value creation and impact.

The idea is that the number of financeable deals in the climate investing industry currently eclipses the amount of capital available to be invested. Conventional capital is moving into the climate investing segment, but with a $125-250 trillion gap, we have room for all comers to benefit. That creates an opportunity to cooperate with others, to drive the benefits and to prevent and manage risks. But at the same time, instances exist where we can, will, and should be in competition. That's healthy—even though it looks a little different than it would in the traditional investing world.

To follow this principal, rely on three critical points:

1. Find like-minded investors;
2. Know your investment model; and
3. Find the gaps that drive success.

When you engage in co-opetition, you build new relationships with like-minded Gigacorn Hunters, which leads you to other strong investment opportunities. You can even expand the breadth and depth of investing syndicates to pool and deploy capital in larger investment opportunities. That could mean you are able to then deploy more capital into more investments more often because you can write smaller checks and spread your capital. When you do this properly, you can better manage the risk profile of your investment portfolio.

Co-opetition also creates a deeper bench when it comes to insights, relationships, and critical skills that can increase the likelihood of a good outcome for you and the companies you invest in.

If you do not collaborate and find yourself investing alone, you will find your deal flow is less robust. You will also limit your access to the additional capital you might need to ensure your investment can thrive between funding rounds and from one round to the next. You will have fewer perspectives around the table, which means less value-adds and fewer co-benefits that can be properly exploited. You won't build relationships with other investors, and you may find that you face a higher concentration of risk, which is not optimal for your investing strategy.

The spirit of co-opetition starts with cooperation and collaboration. That's all about finding other Gigacorn Hunters and establishing relationships that deliver mutual benefit: Benefit for you, the other investors, your common investments, the climate, society and the economy.

Find Like-Minded Investors

I am often asked by individuals who are considering investing in my fund, "Who are your competitors?" I answer honestly...no one. Not yet, anyway.

The climatech industry is so vast, and requires so much capital, that the breadth of opportunity is exceptional. Most people who do invest prefer to work together—to share risk, opportunity, and expertise. Most often, that collaboration comes in the form of syndicates, where individuals are pooling their money together into a single investment opportunity. What might also be considered unique in climatech is a common goal to beat the ticking climate clock while making profits that reward our investors and compel conventional capital out of the destructive elements of the old economy and into the DoE.

When I worked at Nestlé, part of my job was building syndicates. We found that when we collaborated with like-minded investors, our outcomes improved. It wasn't just about pooling our capital and deploying it into larger investments. While that certainly helped, the biggest takeaway was our increase in knowledge, insights, relationships, and skills. We increased the diversity of expertise around the table, and that paid clear dividends.

One of my favorite former colleagues, Tara Carraro, who is currently the Chief Communications Officer at US Steel, once said to me, "Why go to war when you can build a bridge?"

She understood that the most powerful outcomes don't come from fighting for dominance but from collaborating with those who bring different strengths to the table. "When you engage with others as partners, you create opportunities for growth and impact that go far beyond what you could achieve alone."

When looking for an investment partner, you cannot place too much emphasis on how aligned you are in your values and investing philosophy. Each member of the syndicate brings different experiences, insights, and networks, and you should be open to their perspective. They may have solutions to drive greater CRP and enterprise value that you would never have considered. But you have to be sure your end goals are the same, especially if your starting positions are not.

If you're not all aiming in the same direction, it's far too easy for the investment to derail. Be thoughtful about the people with whom you choose to co-invest, and how to stay aligned. Make sure you share not just values, but also respect for governance and management; how companies make, communicate and execute on decisions.

I knew I had found a good group of partners with one fund in which I invested when we faced a moral dilemma: would we say yes to a huge investment from a company that had spent the better part of the past seventy years working to color climate change as a myth?

A Limited Partner Advisory Committee (LPAC) is a committee that provides oversight for a venture capital fund. I was one of a dozen investors to sit on the LPAC of a medium-sized New York-based fund. It was an unusually large committee. We were all committed to climate investment. We were all sustainability executives determined to decrease greenhouse gas emissions, among a few other environmental and social goals. Many of the others had never sat on an LPAC before, but I was confident in our partnership, because we were all aligned in purpose.

Shortly after the fund started, we received a request from an investor wanting to join the fund. It was one of the world's largest oil and gas companies and it had a terrible climate record, going so far as to deny climate change existed and fund anti-climate campaigns for decades. Now, they wanted to refresh their image, and they were hoping we would help them to green-fresh, a term I use for companies that are clearly in the business of climate destructive activity, but trying to paint their actions as environmentally constructive. This is different from greenwashing, which is a tactic intended to hide a company's environmentally destructive activities.

Following a presentation from this potential investor, everyone on the LPAC met to decide whether we should include them. I was surprised, but pleased, to see that the group was unanimously opposed to this oil and gas company joining the fund. We weren't swayed by the size of their substantial investment offer. Collectively, our members had over 150 years working to curb pollution, climate change, and social inequity, and we weren't about to become the green shield for a major polluter. What was equally comforting was the fulsome explanation and response to this oil and gas company. It was not a simple no. It was, "Not now." You see, we wanted to provide motivation for this oil and gas company to act. Let me explain a little more the importance of this distinction.

In the latter part of my high school career and throughout my college years, I worked at and operated restaurants. You can learn a lot about people and motivation toiling behind a bar, apron, and table. Here is a powerful lesson I learned, and I promise it is relevant. Working at a famous restaurant in Toronto called the Pickle Barrel, I had a customer that was very unhappy with his meal. Though he had not mentioned it to me when I came to check on his table during the meal and he cleaned his dinner plate, he complained when I came to offer dessert and coffee. He failed to agree that, even though he had eaten his whole meal, he should pay for it. He asked for the manager. I collected my manager and told him the details as we walked back together to the table. My manager said to me, "Whatever. I'll comp his meal." Where comp means give it to the customer for free…comp is short for complimentary.

When we got back to the table, this is the conversation that took place.

"I should not have to pay for this meal. It was awful. I will never come back to this restaurant," said the customer.

My manager leaned in and replied, "Thank you for letting me know. Since you ate your meal and there is nothing left to inspect, I will not be removing it from the bill. Thank you for your patronage."

The customer was dumbstruck, but he paid his bill and left. At the end of my shift, I asked my manager why he changed his tune. After all, he had told me he was going to comp his meal. What changed? "Simple," he said. "Why would I comp a meal for a customer that is never coming back? There is little need for me to try to make him happy."

This was a lesson in motivation. If the customer had not drawn the hard line, he would have gotten his meal for free.

And so, the LPAC thanked the oil and gas executives and applauded the company's recent public acknowledgment of the science of climate change. Instead of "No," we delivered the message of "Not now" and followed up with an offer. If the oil and gas executives and their company develop and implement a comprehensive climate strategy to which they would commit and publicly disclose, build their climate change bona fides, the LPAC would reconsider.

Our message was received. Several years later, that particular oil and gas company did return and committed a handsome sum to another fund after releasing a comprehensive climate strategy.

When you look for fellow Gigacorn Hunters, make sure you are aligned when it comes to values, objectives and goals, management style, and governance. Then, create an investment model you're all excited to be part of.

Know Your Investment Model

Every fund or asset manager has a financial model to which they try to remain aligned. Your model answers all kinds of questions:

- How many investments are you going to make?
- When are you going to make those investments?
- What's the size of that investment going to look like?
- What percentage of the company do you want to own?
- What's the stage of the investment?
- How much money will the investment need in a follow-on round?
- How many rounds will there be in total?
- How much capital will you reserve for follow on rounds?

It has been my experience that staying disciplined to the model drives success—within reason. You need to know your investment model, but you also need to let that model flex at the right times. Most venture funds are 10-year vehicles, and the market can change quite a bit in that time, so pay attention to market trends and behave accordingly. Catalogue the lessons learned and challenge your fund strategy and thesis often to ensure it is still relevant and effective.

Throughout the investment period—the time capital is deployed from a fund—you will learn a number of valuable lessons. Managing your portfolio for risk means enhancing your financial model with everything you've learned over the course of that investment period. That might include increasing your number of investments (starting with smaller initial investment checks and moving up to fewer and larger investments), or reducing reserves (which frees up additional capital to commit to additional investments).

For instance, let's say that your investment model outlines that you require a 10 percent equity ownership of a company with an investment of

$5 million. You find an opportunity, complete your due diligence and have issued a term sheet, which the company has accepted. Okay, so you are the lead investor and expect to take your 10 percent with $5 million.

You begin to seek co-investors and find a group of like-minded Gigacorn Hunters. Excited, you begin to bring them on board, and you end up co-investing with a larger group with more capital than you predicted coming in. You find, to bring in these other syndicate members your percent equity in the company will need to fall to 8 percent and you need to deploy only $4 million to make that happen.

So what do you do? Well, you don't dig in your heels and say, "Sorry, I can't allow you into the syndicate because my investment model requires me to spend $5 million." No, you assess the value of the syndicate and its membership. Some members may have much deeper pools of capital than you and will be very helpful in the event the company requires an inside funding round.

Other members may want to be a part of the deal so that they can position themselves to lead a subsequent financing thereby increasing the valuation of the company and the returns for you and your fund. So, what do you do? You adjust your model. You end up with a million dollars in your capital pool to deploy on another deal or to reserve for a subsequent round. And the more deals you can do, typically, the more hedged your investment risk.

If you don't have an investment model, it can be hard to weigh the merits of a deal and decide whether it's a good fit for you. When you have that powerful tool, you know what levers you can pull (like bringing on new investors) to flex and improve it. My team and I make a habit of formally reviewing the model every quarter and informally reviewing it weekly as we review market dynamics, the status of the portfolio companies, and the behavior and actions of our syndicate partners. This might include where they are in their investment period, recent raises or investments as well as moves that members of their teams make.

In a large pension fund I advised from 2013-2015, one of our syndicate partners came forward with a proposal: they were interested in taking a significant share of a forthcoming round to which we had committed in our model. The investment was a regional fleet of industrial dry cleaners that, following our investment, had successfully transitioned into an environmentally responsible service provider. Perchloroethylene solvents, which pose health risks, were eliminated from the process, non-toxic detergents were adopted, and investments in water and energy-saving equipment were made. This switch significantly increased margins and attracted new, high-paying customers. The company was growing fast and needed capital to expand to seize the opportunity in front of it.

Considering the deal, we assessed what would happen to our ownership percentage, as well as other implications of this partner leading the next financing round. We found that the valuation this investor wanted to extend was substantially higher than we had modeled. We would lose a small share of our ownership, but the markup, the monetary value of the investment we could claim on our balance sheet, was so substantial that our fund performance was enviable. The concept here is the net gain. Though our percent ownership may have declined, the absolute value of our investment went up significantly. A tidy trade-off.

The deal was clearly a good one, and we agreed to it. We were able to markup the company's valuation substantially and empower the investment with sufficient capital to reach their next set of milestones. At the same time, we were able to release $50 million from our reserve, and use it to advance on a new deal, hedging our portfolio risk.

That was possible because we had a strong model, and we knew how to take advantage of it. Learning to see those deals and even seek them out will push your investment strategy to new levels. And seeking out the right syndicate partners for the right opportunities will take you even further.

Find the Gaps That Drive Success

Every investment opportunity comes with a variety of gaps: in management, strategy, networking, sales, forecasting, customer strategy, market, you name it. I would go so far to say that if you can't find any gaps…well, you know the expression, if it is sounds too good to be true, it is.

Those gaps, if filled, can help increase the likelihood that an investment will be successful. Critically evaluating those gaps opens the playing field. I don't pretend to be an expert in marketing, for example. If I meet a climate investor who is an expert in marketing, that could make them an attractive option to join a syndicate where the investment requires depth in marketing. I do have expertise, however, in decarbonization. When I see a company with a great decarbonization solution that isn't taking full advantage of that benefit, I know that I would be a good addition to their investor slate.

Gigacorn Hunters are active investors, by nature. We seek opportunities to add value. We don't sit on the sidelines and wait for outcomes and for others to make things happen. I very rarely take on a deal if I don't see a way to fill knowledge gaps—a way to create value.

When my fund explored the opportunity to invest in Kuva, we saw a unique platform for mitigating methane emissions. Methane is a particularly nasty greenhouse gas, with one molecule equal to twenty-eight molecules of carbon dioxide in terms of its 100-year global warming potential. For a fund like ClimateIC, anything that can reduce methane emissions is a proposition worth exploring.

Kuva's innovation is, essentially, a high-spectral camera capable of continuously monitoring oil & gas assets from which methane is often emitted. It can identify the source of the emissions and quantify them so that operators can rapidly deploy and eliminate these emissions in real time. At the time of writing this book, no one else can do this or is doing it. A number of solutions are on the market that provide monthly, quarterly or even less frequent monitoring. Can you imagine how much methane is going unnoticed when no one is watching?

When Kuva was presented as a deal option, the largest investor was what is known as a strategic investor. This is typically a corporation with direct knowledge, expertise and relationships that would benefit the investment. In this case, the strategic investor was a muti-billion corporation providing extensive services to the oil & gas sector. It appeared to me and my team that this strategic investor could greatly expand the capability of Kuva to execute on their sales plan. It felt like we would be a good match—and that together, we could help Kuva grow.

For me, the deal was all about co-opetition. We were working with like-minded people, flexing our investment model, and bringing in the experts we needed to fill our knowledge gaps.

When you understand the spirit of co-opetition, you are ready to become a champion for every Gigacorn Hunter out there, and that is what I cover in the next chapter.

Inspire **investors** to become **Gigacorn Hunters** and thus accelerate the transition to the **Decarbonization** of **Everything economy**.

CHAPTER 10

PRINCIPLE 7

BE A CHAMPION

"Never doubt that a small group of thoughtful, committed citizens can change the world; indeed, it's the only thing that ever has."

— Margaret Mead, American anthropologist

A Chorus for Change

When I was in my early thirties, I was the senior manager of Environmental Affairs for a large Canadian financial institution, the Royal Bank of Canada. On behalf of the bank, I was invited to a Day on the Hill, where I, and about ten other leaders from some of Canada's largest corporations, was afforded the opportunity to engage with influential leaders in government about issues of sustainability and business.

At one meeting, our delegation sat down with Mark Carney, the former Governor of the Bank of Canada and the Bank of England. He is one of the world's most regarded former central bankers. At the time I met him he was the Deputy Governor at the Bank of Canada. Each member of the delegation had the opportunity to ask a question of the Deputy Governor. When it was my turn I asked, "What is the

Bank of Canada going to do to help the economy manage climate risk, and help de-risk investments corporate Canada seeks to make to do the same?"

Mark put his hands behind his head, elbows splayed wide and spun his chair around, showing me the back of his head. He said, "The Bank of Canada has no interest in de-risking these types of investments. If you think it's important to invest in it, you'll need to manage the risk."

Fast forward to 2024, and Mark Carney is the UN Special Envoy for Climate Action and Finance and the Co-Chair of the Glasgow Financial Alliance for Net Zero. He is also the Chair of Brookfield Asset Management and Head of Transition Investing. The first fund he helped Brookfield raise, called the Brookfield Transition Fund, is a $12.5 billion decarbonization fund. He is also a sought-after speaker and guest at climate and finance events. He is a modern-day rockstar of climate capitalism.

How did it happen? How did he go from 'climate change is none of our business' to the poster boy for climate and sustainable finance?

I am not saying my question and the ensuing discussion converted him in that room or that he was not already well aware of the principles and impacts of climate risk with his own personal commitment to climate change well developed. However, his response made it clear that it was not something he was ready to engage in on behalf of the Bank of Canada.

I suspect that Mark spent time doing what he has demonstrated makes him unique. Mark has proven to be a listener and diplomat with a capacity to hear, understand and prognosticate—and then communicate with clarity and purpose.

Mark surely saw what we see by meeting with influencers, each of whom would explain their perspective about the connection between economic stability, growth and climate change. This would have armed Mark with the data he needed to obtain his status as one of the world's foremost influencers on the topic of climate risk and sustainable finance, including championing what Gigacorn Hunters like me are trying to do.

Mark showed me that it's easy to convert someone to acknowledge and act appropriately, especially when the scale of weights and measures is loaded with so much scientific evidence and data regarding climate change. All we have to do is stand up and lead the way.

The Gigacorn Army

As a Gigacorn Hunter, you are leading the way. You are pioneering a new economy, the DoE.

The seventh principle of the climate capitalist is to Be a Champion: Inspire investors to become Gigacorn Hunters and thus accelerate the transition to the DoE economy.

The three critical points to consider are:

1. Educate and inspire stakeholders;
2. Empower stakeholders to act; and
3. Market yourself as a Gigacorn Hunter.

I decided some time ago, years ago really, that I would no longer spend time trying to sell the business case for action on decarbonization or sustainability. My theory was that the ability and pace of change of companies and investors that didn't get it, that resisted the science and facts, would mean they would be consigned to history. What I realized, however, was that doing the work—helping companies and investors that did 'get it' increase their alpha and smooth their beta—was, in fact, a compelling way of influencing the DoE.

As investors saw greater returns, I saw the laggards shift. As corporates saw their competitors and leaders adopt climate policies and actions while growing their revenue and influence, others followed.

To successfully transition to this new era, we need strong, influential and engaged stakeholders who can accelerate the investment in and use of climatech. We need them to start and operate climatech companies, champion policy development at both national and international levels, and bring trillions of investment dollars out of the old conventional economy and into the DoE.

We need climate asset managers with trillion-dollar portfolios. We need regulators as high as the President's office, the Prime Minister's office, and the governing and legislative leaderships around the world. We need the academic, the thought leaders and geniuses who understand the need and pathways that can be leveraged to enable decarbonization.

And we need to recruit them all into the Gigacorn army.

If you can help do that, you will help drive the DoE and stimulate economic activity and the creation of well-paying and sustainable employment. You will be a foundational part of enhancing human and ecosystem health and accelerating the transition away from fossil fuels and pollution.

As far as your personal wealth is concerned, you will increase the likelihood that your investments will gain traction and increase in value and returns over time.

If you fail to champion the power and demand of decarbonization, you are only doing half of your job. For years I have been sharing the sentiment, "The time for small moves is over. It's big moves only time."

More recently, I have added that the time for modesty is over. It's time to be bold. We can no longer afford to be spectators or landscapers, as has been the common refrain of those without the authorization or willingness to invest in climatech.

Delaying these investments is not exercising patience; it is failing to recognize that the climate is not patient. It will not wait for you. It will simply swallow your assets, your timber, your roads, bridges and ports, your farms, crops, and buildings, unless you help mitigate the consequences of climate change by investing in the DoE. And remember, this is bigger than climate repair. This is profit, too.

If you're not a champion, you're not helping provide the fodder that the world needs to drive this transition into climatech. And that would be a great loss for us all. Remember, the planet, no matter how poorly we treat it, has billions and billions of years to recover. It deals in geologic time. Humanity is dealing on a very different scale and the way we are emitting carbon means we are accelerating the pace at which we are consuming our allotment. Let me simplify. The Earth has forever, but civilization has only a brief window measured in years to unwind the damage our economy has inflicted.

Educate And Inspire Stakeholders

Evidence is key to influencing stakeholders. Nothing is more compelling than hard data when dealing with rationale people. It is clear, obvious, and factually inarguable. As you build a roster of successful investment examples, this becomes data that you can and should share.

But how?

You need a platform to educate stakeholders, especially those who are impossible to personally reach. How you build it will depend a lot on your own personality. You might choose to participate in conferences, webinars, and local events; lobby politicians; demand your wealth manager or advisor to provide you with climate investing opportunities; or even write your own book, as I am doing here.

Whatever educational material you generate, it should be compelling. It should inspire each stakeholder to act. Think about who you are trying to reach, and what might move them. What do they value most? What issues do they face? Who influences them now, and how can you reach those people as well?

As you seek to inspire and educate, remember to always remain honest. People will hold you and your ideas to account. If you can't back up what you're saying, you will quickly lose credibility. Don't confuse this with opposition, like the recent swirl and politicization of ESG-related investing.

Consider the Texas Pension Fund divestment as an example. In early 2024, Texas legislated that its pension funds must divest themselves of asset managers and instruments that boycott oil and gas, even though it would cost its pensions hundreds of millions of dollars.[78] Or how about the State of Florida where the governor signed an executive order banning state fund managers from considering ESG factors in making investment decisions.[79]

These are simply the last gasps of a dying breed in an industry fighting for its life. Pity them, support them emotionally, but do not embrace them. Rely on facts and data: The rest will take care of itself. It may be two steps forward and one step back for a while, but the gap will widen as we begin to take three steps forward, then four, five, and six.

As my friend and colleague, Simon Mainwaring, CEO of brand consultancy, We First, and global thought leader on sustainability strategy and storytelling, told me:

"By taking action, you inspire and activate the agency of a growing number of stakeholders that together become force multipliers for progress that will usher in the most exciting and transformative renaissance of business in human history."

Be Your Own Champion

After speaking on a panel in San Diego at Sustainable Brands, I was asked by someone who wanted to connect me with his friend: Let's call him Jim. Jim had invested in timberlands in Brazil, and our mutual connection believed he was missing out on a great opportunity to access carbon credits.

We got on a call, and it turned out Jim had invested $40 million in forest lands ripe for harvesting. I walked him through the carbon market opportunity that was in front of him. If he managed this land just a little differently than he was planning, he could sequester a tremendous amount of carbon and monetize that through the carbon market. Here was another opportunity to make more money than the conventional economic model while preserving the natural capital on which the local economy, community, and ecosystem relied.

He was thrilled. I set him up with a carbon project developer, and over three years, they successfully sold millions of tons of carbon credits. One speaking opportunity turned into millions of tons of decarbonization—and a lifelong ally for the Gigacorn army.

Empower Stakeholders to Act

Most influencers stop after they have educated and inspired stakeholders to action. Climate capitalism requires you to go further. You want to provide stakeholders with tools they can use to take action.

What does that look like?

You could provide them an investment opportunity (for my part, I often refer potential new investors to ClimateIC) or the name of an investment seeking private capital or an advisor who specializes in climatech investing. Perhaps you provide specific policy recommendations to elected officials. For entrepreneurs, you can direct them to resources like grant and subsidy programs or incubators and accelerators to help them get a climatech idea off the ground.

From 2021 to 2023, my partners and I tried to engage with the Canadian Government. This included meeting with half a dozen Chiefs of Staff, Deputy Ministers and even the Office of the Prime Minister. We went to each of these meetings armed with actionable tools they could use to supercharge Canada's climate policy.

Most significantly, we outlined how a $5 billion investment in decarbonization could be deployed in a combination of direct deals and indirect fund investments. It would stimulate private capital to accelerate the energy transition. I wasn't acting as a paid consultant, and yes, the plan could directly benefit me if the government allocated some of that capital to my fund. But it was so clearly the right move that it sparked a lot of interest.

We took the time to draft a proposal, including how the investment could be deployed, who would manage it and criteria for selecting investments. The plan ended up in the hands of the Office of the Minister of Finance. I think it is safe to say it got some traction. The next budget included a $15 billion fund called the Canada Growth Fund.

Of course, my partners and I were not the only voices advocating for an investment like this. Dozens of other people were advocating for and championing the idea of a Canadian climate fund. Together, we achieved the critical mass required to help the government move forward.

The more of us who press forward and champion the cause, the more likely we are to engage a stakeholder enough that they act. To make that connection, ask yourself, what do they value most?

- Is it climate change?
- Is it profit?
- Is it protecting their children and the next generation?

- Is it protecting the forest behind their home, or the lake where they vacation?
- Is it winning the next election, or impressing their bosses?

For years people who wanted to influence change through sustainability have asked me the best way to convince people in relation to policies, programs, standards, or actions. My advice has been consistent and not very original, "Meet them where they are. Speak to them in terms they understand. If they are a finance professional speak in terms of Profit & Loss. If they are the CEO of a publicly traded company, speak in terms of share price performance. If they are a statesperson, speak to them in terms of legacy."

Whatever it is, you should pay attention to their motivations, so you can leverage that information to engage in practical, active, and effective engagement strategies and tactics.

I recall one of my earliest attempts to raise capital for a climatech company. After spending countless hours networking, I finally secured a meeting with a wealthy developer—my first one-on-one with someone of truly extraordinary financial means. It felt like a defining moment, and I knew it could shape my approach to future pitches.

We sat on a couch in his spacious office, surrounded by the quiet hum of his assistants at work. After he spent about 20 minutes pressing me with questions about my education, family and ambitions, he turned to me and said, "Well then, what can I do for you?"

"I'd like to understand your perspective on the opportunities emerging in the clean energy transition," I replied.

He leaned back thoughtfully. "You mean climate change? I don't know if it's the right fit for me," he said after a pause. "These issues feel too far in the future and not likely to impact my businesses, and I've built my wealth by focusing on things I can control."

I paused, then responded, "That makes sense. Control is essential—it's how leaders like you get to where you are. But investing in this space isn't about surrendering control; it's about asserting it. Climate change will impact every industry, every market. By leveraging your resources, you can shape the future in ways that align with your values and priorities. Isn't that the ultimate form of control?"

He tilted his head, clearly considering the perspective, but then pushed back. "No. Control is the decisions I can make to ensure the outcomes I want," he asserted, his tone firm.

The room fell silent as his assistants froze, waiting to see where the conversation would go next.

"How many children do you have?" I asked.

"Two," he replied, his tone now more curious than guarded.

"And when the world they inherit faces challenges like heatwaves, food insecurity, disease, and water scarcity, how much control do you think they will have over their choices? If you could make an investment today to secure a sense of control for you and your family tomorrow, why not?"

He didn't invest that day. But several months later, he called me, asking for advice. Over time, I've seen him engage more thoughtfully with the space, and we've stayed in touch ever since.

The lesson? To connect with key stakeholders, you need to engage them as people, not just investors. Often, it's about framing the conversation in ways that resonate with their values and priorities, showing them how action aligns with what matters most to them.

Market Yourself as a Gigacorn Hunter

Very few conventional investors spend time marketing their brand. Why would they need to? Sure, they want to attract capital and build deal flow, but in conventional markets, that has a lot to do with relationships. They have no need for slick websites, or a social media presence. Many are happy to fly under the radar.

Most people don't know what Bessemer Ventures is, even though it is a top venture fund. Many more have heard of Breakthrough Energy, Bill Gates's climate fund.

That's because to succeed, we Gigacorn Hunters must market ourselves. We want to promote the sector and share the opportunities and risks of climate change at large. We are addressing an existential crisis. We're championing the need for capital to be deployed in this sector to accelerate an urgent transition.

When we add the decarbonization purpose to profit, which is the sole ambition of conventional investors, you are obliged to influence others who do not see the opportunity to make huge profits while saving the world. If we don't, the world as we know it will come to a grinding halt. That's a message worth sharing—but no one is going to listen if we can't share our own success stories, as well.

You may find you have one more thing to do when it comes to being a champion. You need to help people spot the distinction between funds that:

- Simply greenwash–the ambition is to leverage the trend of climate change to raise a fund, secure assets to manage and collect fees.

- Have been set up to greenwash for investors–a vehicle set up for a collection of investors seeking to market their green credentials.

- Are the genuine article–dedicated to the transition to the DoE.

Would I like investors to commit to my fund? Absolutely! Would I be excited to know they are committing to other funds driving the DoE?

You know it! But none of us can allow people to make the mistake of investing in funds that fail to meet the Seven Principles of a Climate Capitalist: Measure Carbon, Make Profit, Ensure Demand, Create Value, Find Co-Benefits, Co-opitate (I know, but how else do I translate Co-opetition?) and Be a Champion to drive the decarbonization of the economy.

But what comes next? Put your boots on the ground and start moving forward!

CLOSING

"The best time to plant a tree was twenty years ago. The second best time is now."

— Warren Buffett, Investor and Chairman, Berkshire Hathaway

"Do you think it is too late?"

It was a question I was unprepared for. No one had ever asked me that. It felt invasive, but honest and important. It was 2005 and I was sitting across the table from Melissa Creede, a climate consultant I had met only that day in the nation's capital. We were both attending consultations with the federal government as they were working to design carbon and climate policy for the country.

"What do you mean?" I asked in reply.

"Should we just focus on adapting to the unavoidable consequences of the changing climate, or can we reverse the damage humanity has done to the climate? How can we do that?" she followed.

I took a beat, thought for a moment and said, "This is solvable. I am a climate optimist and know that with the right policy and technology humanity can chart a course toward climate correction."

Getting Started

Now your work can begin.

You've made a valuable commitment by taking the time to read this book. You, like me, are optimistic about what correcting the climate course can do for the environment, society and the economy. You've learned about the Seven Principles for a Climate Investor, and you are primed to become or enhance your skills as a Gigacorn Hunter. I've shared some of my experiences with you, and you have labored through my opinions, facts, and examples. You now understand the opportunities and challenges we and the planet face, and you have the tools to navigate them.

As you reflect on what you've learned, consider the depth of this journey. It's not just about making investments—it's about your legacy and the opportunity you will leave for those who come after you. My purpose, to leverage the capital markets to solve the world's big intractable problems, climate change foremost among them, has guided every step of this journey for me. Your purpose may differ, perhaps it's even bolder or more pointed, but it is the foundation upon which your actions and decisions will rest.

Now, it's your turn to apply all of this to what you do—at home, in school, at work, in politics, in your finances, and in your relationships. But how do you get started? My advice is to first chisel out your purpose by answering this question: "Why am I going to hunt Gigacorns?" Your purpose might be to solve the climate crisis, build a resilient investment portfolio, or even to impress your bosses and secure a bigger bonus at work. Whether your purpose is grounded in a noble pursuit or laser-focused on power, it doesn't matter, as long as you're honest with yourself about why you want to hunt the mighty Gigacorn.

Once you've done that, assess where you are, and identify the levers within your grasp. If you work within a large institutional asset manager, a pension fund, an investment management firm, or another similar entity, the first thing you should do is figure out whether people inside your organization already share your purpose. If so, align with them. Work together to build out a strategy of how you can deploy capital, and where. If not, use what you've learned in this book to get new people on board. Be a champion and spread your message. You'll find people who can be convinced to come onside.

If you already have investment experience, you may want to start your own fund and raise your own capital to deploy using these principles. If you do that, make sure you bring together a team of fellow climate capitalists. You all have to be aligned, and you all have to strive for the same purpose and goal, or you'll get distracted with squirrel opportunities and end up lost in the trees.

If you work in a corporation, meet up with your sustainability team, which should be identifying the impacts that your organization influences or has contributed toward in its past, and figure out how you can solve some of those challenges through investing. You may even be able to take some of your corporate funds and dedicate them to investing in climate solutions. Perhaps establish a corporate venture fund.

If you have capital to deploy, seek out funds that are doing work that aligns with your purpose. My fund, ClimateIC, is only one example—so many people are out there doing good work in finance, research, and advocacy. I've included a list of some of those in the Resources section at the back of the book.

Whether you have a large or modest amount of capital, opportunities are out there for you. If you have someone who manages your retirement money, you can engage with them and encourage them to follow my seven principles.

If you only have a few thousand dollars—or even just a few hundred—check out crowdfunding websites like Kickstarter and Indiegogo and find solutions where people are looking for small individual investments. No matter how small or large the investment, the principles remain the same. Do not underestimate the power of a modest investment. The great successes happen when a critical mass of support gets behind a good idea. Your investment could be just what is needed to tip the scale in favor of the DoE.

If you are building a fund or choosing one to invest in, think about the specific areas where you want to focus. My fund focuses on the UN IPCC Six—the six sectors of the economy from which all anthropogenic emissions are derived. Is there a sector or a sub-sector that you think you can significantly influence or impact? You may have connections, relationships, or other levers at your disposal that make one sector more appealing than others. Ask yourself, "What's the mechanism by which I can actually deploy that capital or influence change?"

As you move forward, it's important to remember that this journey is not just about making an investment—it's about tracking the outcome. Once you've deployed your capital, make sure you track your performance. Measure the decarbonization impact of your fund or investment, as well as the profit. You need to assess, "Is it delivering the outcome that I thought it would and should?" This ongoing measurement will allow you to iterate, learn, and improve your future investments.

It will also allow you to advocate for the success of Gigacorn hunting and carbon investing.

Sharing your story, your ambition, your approaches, and your successes is crucial. When you do, you will recruit more soldiers for the Gigacorn hunting army. You will inspire the next generation to pursue Gigacorn hunting dreams.

And remember, it is okay if you cannot invest. Every one of us is of different means and has different priorities. But we can all advocate, and we can all be champions.

A Family Legacy

I've seen the strength of the story we're sharing in my own family. In 2023, my oldest son turned sixteen. We were sitting together around the dinner table, and my wife asked him about his course selection for the following school year. He would be in 11th grade, and he had to start homing in on what he wanted to study in university, so he could take the right prerequisites in high school.

He looked over at me and smiled nervously. "Well, I kind of want to do what Dad does," he admitted. "I want to work in sustainability. So, I guess I have to start looking more at the science and math stuff." Then he added, "I mean, there's this thing you can do, where instead of taking it in the classroom, you can do 11th grade science over the summer…at the Huntsman Marine Center in New Brunswick."

I was floored, though I tried not to show my excitement. In that moment, I felt warmth and connection with my son. The Huntsman Marine Center was where I had laid down in the seaweed and experienced my inspired moment, that flipping of the switch that made me change career paths from medical doctor to sustainability professional. I thought of that moment, of the sun rising across the water, and I knew how powerful my son would find his own moment of connection or catharsis. It was an incredible opportunity.

"Why do you want to do that?" I asked him.

"I guess you made me realize…I can do this for a living. Saving the planet doesn't have to just be a dream, or a passion, or whatever. It can be something real. A career."

As I saw him sitting across from me, fully his own person and yet inspired by the same things that inspired me, I felt a wild surge of hope. I saw that the next generation is coming to the same realization I did, but so much earlier. It isn't just about hope for them: it's about action. We have helped steward this cultural transition of a critical mass of interested intellect. That will help us drive decarbonization, and the sustainable future. The change is coming. They're ready for it.

You must be ready, too.

We are in the middle of one of the biggest transformations the world has ever seen. It is a translocation of capital, of how we make things, how we use things, and how we handle things. These principles are here to help you do more than just make exceptional decarbonization investments to help accelerate the transition. They're also your talking points. They're a series of stories, both defensive and offensive, that you can use when you need to confront those who still find themselves stuck in the conventional way of operating.

You have the proof. You have the process. You have the fiduciary duty you need to give yourself the confidence to start Gigacorn Hunting.

I mentioned earlier in the book one of the arguments that I hear from people who are resistant to change. You remember. Sentiments like "We're landscaping right now. We're adjusting the foundations, and we'll be ready to plant soon."

To them, I say, "Isn't it wonderful to believe that you have all this time to be patient? You know what's not patient? The climate." And if the fate of society isn't a compelling enough reason, remember this. If you sit back and wait, you will miss the opportunity that comes with acting at the right time. You will find yourself just like those at the end of the tech boom, watching the meteoric success of those around you and wondering how you missed out. If you missed it the first time around, it was because you didn't have the knowledge and expertise you needed to make the right investment decisions.

But you have that now.

You have understanding, and that should bring you courage. Change is never easy. And changing other people's minds is even tougher. But there's no more time to delay. You have a roadmap, and everything you need to follow it. Use this book as your framework, to guide yourself and others on the path of climate capitalism.

And if you have questions or concerns, I want to be available as a resource for you. Connect with me. Go to my website, connect on LinkedIn, send me a message. We can discuss any and all of the options that might be available to you, whether it's direct investment in my fund, establishing your own fund, or even bringing me in to speak to your managers or investors to help them see the light. I'm available as a resource and a sounding board for your investment strategies. Remember, we need to support each other and build a network of inspired Gigacorn Hunters. That's the path to real success.

We are becoming the mainstream. Investing with purpose for profit is no longer the strategy of an outside group of agitators. It is a highly profitable methodology that brings with it the promise of a bright, sustainable future. A future that is environmentally restorative, socially equitable, and prosperous.

I've shared a number of examples of potential investments throughout this book. No doubt each of you have seen, and will continue to see, dozens, if not hundreds or even thousands, of potential Gigacorns. Use these principles to find yours, to fund them, and to help each grow. Remember, we need only sixty to reach a net zero economy.

We can't let up. And with the opportunities in front of us…why would we ever want to?

Let's go hunting.

RESOURCES

There is no shortage of information available to guide you on your Gigacorn hunting journey. I've taken the time to compile a series of resources that can help keep you informed and provide essential data, from foundational insights to more sophisticated analysis. These resources are intended to assist you in expanding your knowledge, conducting due diligence, and building connections in climate investing. Below is a curated list of references I frequently use, along with a selection of conferences to consider attending, should you wish to immerse yourself further in this space.

Think Tanks, Associations, and Not-for-Profits:

1. **Ceres** (https://www.ceres.org): Advocates for sustainability in business through leadership and policies.

2. **Climate Action 100+** (https://www.climateaction100.org): Investor-led initiative pushing corporate climate responsibility.

3. **Climate Policy Initiative** (https://www.climatepolicyinitiative.org): Supports effective energy and climate policies globally.

4. **Forum for the Future** (https://www.forumforthefuture.org): Promotes systemic change for sustainability.

5. **International Energy Agency (IEA)** (https://www.iea.org): Provides energy data, analysis, and policy recommendations.

6. **International Institute for Sustainable Development (IISD)** (https://www.iisd.org): Focuses on sustainability and economic development strategies.

7. **International Investors Group on Climate Change (IIGCC)** (https://www.iigcc.org): Investor group advocating for climate-resilient investments.

8. **Institutional Limited Partners Association (ILPA) Decarbonization Handbook** (https://ilpa.org/resource/decarbonisation-handbook-for-lps/): A guide for limited partners on decarbonization strategies.

9. **Net Zero Asset Owner Alliance** (https://www.unepfi.org/net-zero-alliance/): Coalition committing to net-zero investment portfolios by 2050.

10. **Rocky Mountain Institute** (https://rmi.org): Accelerates clean energy transitions through research and action.

11. **World Resources Institute (WRI)** (https://www.wri.org): Researches sustainable natural resources and climate solutions.

12. **World Business Council for Sustainable Development (WBCSD)** (https://www.wbcsd.org): Helps businesses adopt sustainability practices.

13. **The Climate Group** (https://www.theclimategroup.org): Accelerates climate action by engaging governments and businesses.

14. **United Nations Environment Program (UNEP)** (https://www.unep.org): Coordinates international environmental activities and solutions.

15. **United Nations Environment Program Finance Initiative (UNEP FI)** (https://www.unepfi.org): Mobilizes financial institutions to tackle climate challenges.

16. **United Nations Sustainable Development Goals** (https://sdgs.un.org/goals): Global blueprint for achieving a better, sustainable future.

Standards:

1. **American Carbon Registry (ACR)** (https://acrcarbon.org): Carbon offset standard and registry for voluntary markets.

2. **Climate Action Reserve (CAR)** (https://www.climateaction-reserve.org): Develops standards and registers carbon offset projects.

3. **Gold Standard Foundation** (https://www.goldstandard.org): Certifies high-integrity carbon reduction projects.

4. **Greenhouse Gas Protocol (GHG Protocol)** (https://ghgpro-tocol.org): Provides guidelines for greenhouse gas accounting.

5. **IFRS Foundation** (https://www.ifrs.org): Develops global accounting standards, now integrating sustainability.

6. **Partnership for Carbon Accounting Financials (PCAF)** (https://carbonaccountingfinancials.com): Standardizes carbon accounting for financial institutions.

7. **Principles for Responsible Investment (PRI)** (https://www.unpri.org): Promotes sustainable investment practices globally.

8. **Science Based Targets Initiative** (https://sciencebasedtargets.org): Guides companies on setting emissions reduction targets.

9. **Task Force on Climate-Related Financial Disclosures** (https://www.fsb-tcfd.org): Provides a framework for climate risk reporting.

10. **The Integrity Council for the Voluntary Carbon Market** (https://icvcm.org): Ensures high standards for voluntary carbon markets.

11. **Verra** (https://verra.org): Administers carbon certification programs like the Verified Carbon Standard.

Newsletters:

1. **Axios Generate** (https://www.axios.com/signup/generate): Daily energy and climate news updates.

2. **Bloomberg New Energy Finance** (https://about.bnef.com): Provides data-driven insights into energy trends.

3. **Climate Technology Venture Capital (CTVC) by Sightline** (https://www.ctvc.co): Tracks climate tech investments and innovations.

4. **Canary Media** (https://www.canarymedia.com): Independent news on the energy transition.

5. **Carbon Brief** (https://www.carbonbrief.org): Reports on the latest climate science and policy developments.

6. **Carbon Herald** (https://carbonherald.com): Provides updates on the carbon market and offset trends.

7. **Clean Energy Wire** (https://www.cleanenergywire.org): In-depth journalism on energy policy and climate change.

8. **Climate Hack Weekly** (https://news.climatehack.global): Weekly news about climate matters, and transactions.

9. **Inside Climate News** (https://insideclimatenews.org): Climate change news and investigative reporting.

10. **Last Week in Climate** (https://www.lastweek.inclimate.com): Weekly recap of major climate developments.

11. **The Breakthrough Institute** (https://thebreakthrough.org): Research on technological solutions for environmental problems.

12. **Trellis** (https://trellis.net): Data and insights on climate technology investments.

Data & Research Sources:

1. **Carbon180** (https://carbon180.org): Advocates for carbon removal solutions through policy and innovation.

2. **Carbon Removal Policy Tracker** (https://tracker.carbon-gap.org): Tracks carbon removal policies and projects across Europe.

3. **CCUS Map** (https://ccusmap.com): Tracks global carbon capture, utilization, and storage projects.

4. **CDR.fyi** (https://www.cdr.fyi): Tracks carbon dioxide removal project progress.

5. **Cleantech Group** (https://www.cleantech.com): Insights and data on clean technology innovation.

6. **Climate Action Tracker** (https://climateactiontracker.org): Tracks national progress toward climate targets.

7. **Climate Change Laws of the World** (https://climate-laws.org): Database of global climate legislation and policies.

8. **Climate Impact Lab** (https://impactlab.org): Data on the economic impact of climate change.

9. **Climate Trace** (https://www.climatetrace.org): Tracks global greenhouse gas emissions using satellite data.

10. **CRANE** (https://cranetool.org): Tools for evaluating carbon removal project viability.

11. **En-Roads Climate Pathway Simulator** (https://en-roads.climateinteractive.org): Models climate policy impacts in real time.

12. **Grantham Research Institute on Climate Change** (https://www.lse.ac.uk/granthaminstitute/): Research on climate change economics and policy.

13. **National Oceanographic and Atmospheric Administration** (https://www.noaa.gov): Provides climate and atmospheric data.

Conferences (in order by calendar):

1. **World Economic Forum** (weforum.org): Global platform for public-private collaboration and economic discussions.

2. **Cleantech Forum** (cleantech.com): Focuses on sustainable innovation, cleantech investments, and climate technologies.

3. **GreenBiz** (greenbiz.com): Brings together leaders on sustainability, circular economy, and ESG.

4. **CERAWeek** (ceraweek.com): Major energy conference exploring the future of energy and technology.

5. **World Agritech Summit** (worldagritechusa.com): Advances in agricultural technology to improve food and sustainability.

6. **Innovation Zero** (innovationzero.com): Climate tech expo focusing on decarbonization and sustainable solutions.

7. **NREL Cleantech Industry Forum** (nrel.gov): Accelerates cleantech commercialization with industry and research collaboration.

8. **Milken Institute Global Conference** (milkeninstitute.org): Global economic discussions on health, finance, and sustainability initiatives.

9. **Carbon Unbound** (carbonunbound.com): Conference focused on scaling carbon removal technologies and innovations.

10. **Responsible Business Summit** (reutersevents.com): ESG-driven conference on responsible business practices and sustainability.

11. **Economist Sustainability Week** (economistimpact.com): Explores sustainability issues, climate challenges, and economic impacts.

12. **CleanAI Summit** (cleanaisummit.com): Focuses on AI innovations for climate and environmental sustainability.

13. **Aspen Ideas Festival** (aspenideas.org): Forum for discussing big ideas in politics, science, and culture.

14. **World Water Week** (worldwaterweek.org): Tackles global water issues, sustainability, and related challenges.

15. **NY Climate Week** (climateweeknyc.org): Annual event driving climate action and sustainability leadership.

16. **Sustainable Brands** (sustainablebrands.com): Business conference focused on sustainability, branding, and innovation.

17. **VERGE** (greenbiz.com/events/verge): Explores climate tech and sustainability for business and infrastructure.

18. **Conference of the Parties (COP)** (unfccc.int/cop): UN conference on climate change negotiations and global agreements.

19. **MaRS Climate Conference** (marsdd.com): Innovations in climate tech, sustainability, and entrepreneurial ventures.

ACKNOWLEDGMENTS

To my incredible wife, Karen—the love of my life and my constant muse. For more than twenty years, you have inspired me to be my best self, and your unwavering love and support have made this book possible. I could not have done it without you. And to my boys, Noah Leaf and Ethan Rain—thank you for your humor, your insatiable quest for meaning and knowledge, and for keeping us all close to, but on the right side of the line of chaos.

Thank you also to my parents, my parents-in-law, and my friends and family who encouraged me throughout the book writing process. Thank you to my team at ClimateIC including my partners Kevin Kimsa and Paul Atkinson, and Zoe Best, Leanne Bogusky, Adam Fell, Jackie Manley, Lilliana Paoletti and Ariel Sharir.

A heartfelt thank you to Karen Strauss at Hybrid Global Publishing and Helen Chang—your expertise and dedication made this book a reality. Also, to my research assistant, Natasha Czegledy without whom the starting line may never have been found.

There are so many others to thank—those who encouraged, inspired, educated, counseled, supported, and challenged me, those who took a chance on me, and those who let me stand on their shoulders and sleep on their couch, including: Peter and Joyce Budd, Gary Saunders, Brett Etkin, Shari Austin, Lynn Patterson, Peter Koch, Mike Harris, Tim Brown, Fernando Merce, Tara Carraro, Afdhel Aziz, Will Sarni, Antonella Penta, Phil Haid, Gil Eiges, Elaine Pile, Sean Pile,

Pete MacDonald, Sarah Manos, Mitch Abrams, Courtney Budd and Wally Slocki.

And to anyone I may have unintentionally missed—please know your support, encouragement, and contributions have not gone unnoticed. You've played an important role in this journey, and I am grateful.

REFERENCES

1 **Enphase Energy, Inc.** "Enphase Energy Inc - Climate Change 2023." CDP Climate Change Questionnaire, 2023

2 **Intergovernmental Panel on Climate Change (IPCC).** *Climate Change 2022: Mitigation of Climate Change.* Contribution of Working Group III to the Sixth Assessment Report of the IPCC. Cambridge University Press. 2022.

3 Data compiled from reports including: **Cleantech Group.** *2014 Global Cleantech 100 Report: Profiling the Companies Delivering Sustainable Innovation* Cleantech Group, 2014; and **Cambridge Associates.** *Clean Tech Company Performance Statistics.* Cambridge Associates, 2019.

4 **United Nations Framework Convention on Climate Change (UNFCCC).** *Adoption of the Paris Agreement.* Paris Agreement, 21st Conference of the Parties (COP21), December 2015.

5 PwC. (2022). **State of Climate Tech 2022: The Next Frontier for Venture Capital.**

6 International Monetary Fund. (2021). **Global Financial Stability Report: Climate Change—Physical Risk and Equity Prices.** International Monetary Fund.

7 McKinsey & Company. (2022). **The Net-Zero Transition: What It Would Cost, What It Could Bring.** McKinsey Global Institute.

8 **PwC. (2023).** *State of Climate Tech 2023: Scaling Climate Tech for a Net Zero Future.* PricewaterhouseCoopers.

9 PwC & National Venture Capital Association (NVCA). (2023). *MoneyTree Report: Q2 2023*. PricewaterhouseCoopers & National Venture Capital Association.

10 **CB Insights. (2023).** *State of Climate Tech: Climate Tech Resilience in a Shifting Investment Landscape.* CB Insights.

11 **PitchBook. (2023).** *PitchBook Sustainable Investment Report: Q2 2023.* PitchBook Data, Inc.

12 **Silicon Valley Bank (now part of First Citizens Bank). (2023).** *Climate Tech Investment Trends Report.* First Citizens Bank.

13 **HolonIQ. (2023).** *Global Climate Tech 1000 Report.* HolonIQ.

14 **pv magazine.** (2023). Solar Levelized Cost of Electricity is 29% Lower Than Any Fossil Fuel Option. pv magazine.

15 **International Monetary Fund (IMF). (2023).** *Fossil Fuel Subsidies by Country and Global Trends.* International Monetary Fund.

16 **U.S. Department of Energy. (2022).** *Solid-State Lighting: 2022 Suggested Research Topics Supplement.* U.S. Department of Energy.

17 **NielsenIQ. (2023).** *The Evolution of Sustainability in CPG: Shoppers Continue to Seek Environmentally Friendly Products.* NielsenIQ.

18 **Amazon. (2020).** *Amazon Announces the Climate Pledge Fund to Invest in Companies Building Products, Services, and Technologies to Help Fight Climate Change.*

19 **Microsoft. (2020).** *Microsoft Will Be Carbon Negative by 2030.* Microsoft Official Blog.

20 **Walmart. (2020).** *Project Gigaton: Walmart's Commitment to Reduce One Billion Metric Tons of Emissions by 2030.* Walmart.

21 **International Energy Agency (IEA). (2022).** *Global EV Outlook 2022.* International Energy Agency.

22 **International Energy Agency (IEA). (2021).** *Global EV Outlook 2021.* International Energy Agency.

23   **Intergovernmental Panel on Climate Change (IPCC). (2022).** *Sixth Assessment Report: Impacts, Adaptation and Vulnerability.* IPCC.

24   **Insurance Bureau of Canada (IBC). (2023).** *2023 Wildfire Season: Billions in Insured Losses Across Key Sectors.* Insurance Bureau of Canada.

25   **Pacific Gas and Electric Company (PG&E). (2019).** *PG&E Corporation and Pacific Gas and Electric Company File for Reorganization Under Chapter 11.* Pacific Gas and Electric.

26   **Royal Dutch Shell. (2021).** *Shell Announces Significant Write-Down of Oil and Gas Assets Amid Energy Transition Plans.* Shell Press Release.

27   **The Coca-Cola Company. (2021).** *Annual Report: Adapting to Climate Change and Supply Chain Risks.* The Coca-Cola Company.

28   **The Coca-Cola Company. (2021).** *Annual Report: Adapting to Climate Change and Supply Chain Risks.* The Coca-Cola Company.

29   **Brookfield Asset Management. (2021).** *Brookfield Announces Launch of $15 Billion Global Transition Fund.* Brookfield Asset Management.

30   **TPG. (2021).** *TPG Closes $7.3 Billion Rise Climate Fund to Drive Climate Solutions.* TPG.

31   **Lowercarbon Capital. (2022).** *Lowercarbon Capital Raises $800 Million to Back Climate Tech Startups.* Lowercarbon Capital.

32   **BlackRock. (n.d.).** BlackRock-Temasek Sustainability Initiatives. BlackRock.

33   **National Oceanic and Atmospheric Administration (NOAA). (2023).** *Trends in Atmospheric Carbon Dioxide: Global Monthly Mean CO_2.* NOAA Earth System Research Laboratory.

34   **National Aeronautics and Space Administration (NASA). (2021).** *Thwaites Glacier: Antarctic Doomsday Glacier Under Threat from Warm Water.* NASA Earth Observatory.

35 **Royal Meteorological Society. (2022).** *The Azores High: How an Atmospheric High-Pressure System Affects European Weather Patterns.* Royal Meteorological Society.

36 **U.S. Bureau of Reclamation. (2022).** *Lake Mead Water Levels and the Impact of Drought on Hydropower Production.* U.S. Department of the Interior.

37 **U.S. Geological Survey (USGS). (2022).** *Melting Permafrost and Its Impact on Infrastructure in the Arctic.* U.S. Geological Survey.

38 **Intergovernmental Panel on Climate Change (IPCC). (2021).** *Sixth Assessment Report: Impacts of Climate Change on Human Health.* IPCC.

39 **Food and Agriculture Organization of the United Nations (FAO). (2022).** *The State of Food Security and Nutrition in the World: Rising Food Prices Due to Climate Change and Supply Disruptions.* FAO.

40 **World Meteorological Organization (WMO). (2023).** *WMO Atlas of Mortality and Economic Losses from Weather, Climate and Water Extremes (1970–2021).* World Meteorological Organization.

41 **Lee, A. (2013).** *Welcome to the Unicorn Club: Learning from Billion-Dollar Startups.* TechCrunch.

42 **CB Insights. (2023).** *The Complete List of Unicorn Companies.* CB Insights.

43 **Climate Policy Initiative (CPI). (2024).** *Global Landscape of Climate Finance 2024.* Climate Policy Initiative.

44 **World Commission on Environment and Development (WCED). (1987).** *Our Common Future (Brundtland Report).* Oxford University Press.

45 **PwC. (2023).** *State of Climate Tech 2023: Climate Tech Investment Trends and Performance.* PwC.

46 **BloombergNEF. (2023).** *Climate Tech Outlook 2023: How Climate Investments Are Outpacing Traditional Sectors.* Bloomberg New Energy Finance.

47 **McKinsey & Company. (2022).** *The Net-Zero Transition: How Investors Can Capture Opportunities.* McKinsey Global Institute.

48 **International Energy Agency (IEA). (2022).** *Clean Energy Investing: Trends and Opportunities in 2023.* IEA.

49 **Intergovernmental Panel on Climate Change (IPCC). (2018).** *Global Warming of 1.5°C: An IPCC Special Report on the Impacts of Global Warming of 1.5°C Above Pre-Industrial Levels.* IPCC.

50 **Intergovernmental Panel on Climate Change (IPCC). (2018).** *Global Warming of 1.5°C: An IPCC Special Report on the Impacts of Global Warming of 1.5°C Above Pre-Industrial Levels.* IPCC.

51 **World Resources Institute & World Business Council for Sustainable Development. (2004).** *The Greenhouse Gas Protocol: A Corporate Accounting and Reporting Standard (Revised Edition).*

52 **U.S. Department of Energy. (2021).** *Grid Modernization Initiative: Ensuring Reliability and Resilience in the Power Grid.* U.S. Department of Energy.

53 **Federal Energy Regulatory Commission (FERC). (2023).** *Energy Infrastructure Update: Renewable Energy's Growing Share of U.S. Electric Generation Capacity.* Federal Energy Regulatory Commission.

54 **National Public Radio (NPR). (2021).** *California Wildfires Are Now the Largest Source of Carbon Emissions in the State.* NPR.

55 Box, G. E. P., & Draper, N. R. (1987). *Empirical Model-Building and Response Surfaces.* Wiley.

56 **Task Force on Climate-related Financial Disclosures (TCFD). (2021).** *2021 Status Report: The Benefits of Climate Risk Disclosure on Decarbonization Efforts.* Financial Stability Board.

57 **Finavera Renewables. (2013).** *Corporate Transition and Rebranding: Challenges in the Renewable Energy Sector.* Finavera Renewables Press Release.

58 **CB Insights. (2023).** *State of Climate Tech: Investment Trends in the Climate Tech Sector.* CB Insights.

59 **BlackRock. (2022).** *BlackRock Reports Fourth Quarter 2022 Earnings and Full Year Results.* BlackRock, Inc.

60 **Fink, L. (2022).** *Larry Fink's 2022 Letter to CEOs: The Power of Capitalism.* BlackRock.

61 **United Nations Environment Programme Finance Initiative (UNEP FI). (2005).** *A Legal Framework for the Integration of Environmental, Social, and Governance Issues into Institutional Investment: The Freshfields Report.* UNEP Finance Initiative.

62 **BP, Royal Dutch Shell, and others. (2020).** *Oil Majors Announce Significant Write-Downs Amid Energy Transition.* Financial Times.

63 **Gaddy, B., Sivaram, V., & O'Sullivan, F. (2016).** *Venture Capital and Cleantech: The Wrong Model for Clean Energy Innovation.* MIT Energy Initiative.

64 **Gaddy, B., Sivaram, V., & O'Sullivan, F. (2016).** *Venture Capital and Cleantech: The Wrong Model for Clean Energy Innovation.* MIT Energy Initiative.

65 **European Commission. (2021).** *Global Methane Pledge: Reducing Global Methane Emissions by 30% by 2030.* European Commission Press Release.

66 **United Nations Environment Programme (UNEP). (2021).** *Global Methane Assessment: Benefits and Costs of Mitigating Methane Emissions.* UNEP.

67 **Supreme Court of the United States. (2024).** *Loper Bright Enterprises v. Raimondo.* Case No. 22-451.

68   The White House. (2022). *The Inflation Reduction Act of 2022.* The White House.

69   uropean Commission. (2020). *A European Green Deal: Striving to be the First Climate-Neutral Continent.* European Commission.

70   Government of Canada. (2022). *Canada Growth Fund: Supporting the Transition to a Low-Carbon Economy.* Government of Canada.

71   Keller, T. (2019). *The French Laundry, Per Se: Thomas Keller's Reflections on Culinary Art.* Artisan Books.

72   Integrity Council for the Voluntary Carbon Market (ICVCM). (2023). *Core Carbon Principles and Assessment Framework.*

73   Financial Times. (2023). *Big Companies Move Away from Carbon Offsets to Cut Emissions in Supply Chains.* Financial Times.

74   Bloomberg. (2023). *Carbon Giants Like South Pole Accused of Overstating Climate Benefits in Offset Projects.* Bloomberg Businessweek.

75   S&P Global Commodity Insights. (2023). *Price slump in 2023 clouds outlook for voluntary carbon market.*

76   United Nations. (2015). *Transforming Our World: The 2030 Agenda for Sustainable Development.* United Nations General Assembly.

77   U.S. Department of Agriculture (USDA). (2021). *A Renewed Focus on Soil Carbon.* USDA Climate Hubs.

78   WFAA. (2024). *Texas divestment over reduced oil and gas involvement could cost state hundreds of millions, report says.*

79   S&P Global Market Intelligence. (2022). *Florida adopts anti-ESG rule for state's $186B pension plan.*

INDEX

A

Afforestation, Reforestation, and Revegetation (ARR) projects, 108
Agenda for Sustainable Development, 120. *See also* Sustainable Development Goals
Air Company, 111–113
Airbnb, 30
Algonquin Provincial Park, 32
Amazon, 19, 70, 85
Apple, 70, 131
Applied Ventures, 4
Aqua Membrane, 5
Arctic, 24
Atkinson, Paul, 8, 9, 35
Azores High, 24

B

Bank of Canada. *See* Royal Bank of Canada
Bank of England, 145
batteries, 5, 16, 127
Berkshire Hathaway, 22
Bessemer Ventures, 155
Bezos, Jeff, 96
BlackRock, 23, 78
Bloomberg Businessweek, 108
BloombergNEF, 49
Box, George, 59
Breakthrough Energy, 155
Brookfield Asset Management, 23, 146
Brookfield Transition Fund, 146
Budd, Peter, 117
Buffett, Warren, 157

C

CalSTRS, 22
Cambridge Associates, 16,
carbon accounting, 52, 64, 107
carbon capture & utilization (CCU), 111, 112
carbon dioxide, atmospheric, 4, 9, 23–24, 111–112
Carbon Dioxide Equivalents (CO_2e), 25
carbon insets, 105, 107
Carbon Investment Efficiency (CIE), *See also* Minimum Carbon Investment Efficiency (mCIE), 52, 55, 56, 58, 59, 60
carbon offsets and credits, 105–108, 109, 111
Carbon Reduction Intensity (CRI), 52, 53, 56
Carbon Reduction Potential (CRP), 52–60, 62, 63, 65, 66, 84, 90, 102, 103, 113, 114–115, 119, 120, 123, 124, 129, 135
measuring, 48–49
models for, 57–58
Carney, Mark, 145–146
Carraro, Tara, 134–135
CB Insights, 17, 77
Chevron Doctrine, 94
CleanFiber, 5
Cleantech 1.0, 86–87
cleantech, 4, 8, 15
Climate capitalism, 42, 48, 59, 66, 103, 132, 147
Climate change mitigation, 7, 121
climate credits, 109–110
Climate Pledge Arena, 19

Unilever, 107
Union Square Ventures, 23
United Nations (UN), 16, 50, 99, 119
United Nations Framework Convention
    on Climate Change (UNFCCC), 16
United Nations Intergovernmental Panel
    on Climate Change (UN IPCC), 9,
    50, 51, 124, 160
United Nations Sustainable Development
    Goals. *See* Sustainable Development
    Goals
UN IPCC Six, 160
United States Environmental Protection
    Agency (EPA), 94
United States Supreme Court, 94
U. S. Steel, 134

V

value, quantifying, 109–113
value creation. *See* creating value
VC. *See* venture capital

venture capital, 3, 11, 60, 86, 135. *See also*
    National Venture Capital Association,
    specific firms

W

Walmart, 19
Waste Management, Inc., 97
Watchman, Paul, 79
water
    filtration, 125
    infiltration, 124
    scarcity, 24, 25, 154
    sector, 126
    use, reduction, 45, 91, 124, 140
Watson, Thomas, 83
weather. *See* extreme weather events
wind power, 56, 72, 123
World Meteorological Organization
    (WMO), 25

www.ingramcontent.com/pod-product-compliance
Lightning Source LLC
Chambersburg PA
CBHW062132040426

42335CB00039B/2080